P9-DEE-943

Rethinking Adult Religious Education

A Practical Parish Guide

Karen Ann Szentkeresti
Jeanne Tighe

PAULIST PRESS
New York/Mahwah

The publisher gratefully acknowledges the use of: excerpts from *Sharing the Light of Faith*, National Catechetical Directory for Catholics of the United States, copyright © 1979, by the United States Catholic Conference, Department of Education, Washington, D.C. used by permission of the copyright owner. All rights reserved; material adapted from *Teaching Teachers to Teach* by Donald & Patricia Griggs, copyright © 1974 by Griggs Educational Services, are used by permission of the publisher, Abingdon Press; material from *The Modern Practice of Adult Education* by Malcom Knowles is reprinted by permission of Cambridge, The Adult Education Company, N.Y.; graphics from *Teaching Religion Effectively* by Mary K. Cove and Jane Regan Trep, © 1982, are used by permission of W.C. Brown Publishers, Iowa.

Copyright © 1986 by
Jeanne Tighe and Karen Szentkeresti

All rights reserved. No part of this book may be reproduced or transmitted in any form or by any means, electronic or mechanical, including photocopying, recording or by any information storage and retrieval system without permission in writing from the Publisher.

Library of Congress
Catalog Card Number: 86-61760

ISBN: 0-8091-2829-2

Published by Paulist Press
997 Macarthur Boulevard
Mahwah, New Jersey 07430

Printed and bound in the
United States of America

CONTENTS

Lincoln Christian College

ABOUT THE AUTHORS

Karen Ann Szentkeresti presently serves as a member of St. Mary Magdalene's Pastoral Team in Willowick, Ohio. She formerly served as a consultant in religious education for the Cleveland diocese with a focus on parish religious education program development and the on-going formation of catechists and administrators. She received her M.A. in religious education from John Carroll University. Karen has been involved in parish ministry serving as a parish director of religious education and a teacher on the child, youth, and adult levels. She has facilitated sacramental programs, family and youth retreats, adult education courses, and interfaith sharing sessions. Her publications include articles in *Catechist* and *Spirit and Life* magazines, various newsletters, and newspapers on catechesis and spirituality.

Jeanne Tighe presently serves as adult education director for Gesu Parish in Cleveland, Ohio. She has taught at Ursuline College and John Carroll University. Jeanne received her M.A. in religious education from John Carroll University. Her experiences include over twenty years of teaching in parochial and parish schools of religion. She has served on diocesan committees for curriculum development and worked the past fourteen years in religious education programs for pre-school through adult education. Her work includes administration and program management. Publications in those areas have appeared in *P.A.C.E.* magazine. She has facilitated teacher training programs and conducted sacramental programs, youth and adult retreats and family enrichment opportunities. Jeanne is a resident of Solon, Ohio.

We dedicate this work
to all those who have journeyed with us in faith,
supporting us with their love
and inspiring us with their lives:

Our parents:
William and Rita Szentkeresti
William and Louise Tighe

*Our friends and all those who have contributed
so richly to this mutual adventure:*

Beverly Ann Belock, S.I.W.
Dianne Selva, S.F.C.C.
Thomas Cousineau
Dr. Ray R. Noll
Jean Cruttenden Noll
Jan and Pete Fuldauer

Foreword

The fact that you are reading this book suggests a desire on your part to deepen your understanding of adult religious education. No doubt you brought with you some questions, needs, feelings, and dreams for adult education in your own life, in your parish community, and in the Church at large. It might be helpful to stop and jot down your questions, needs, feelings, and dreams. They are valuable resources and can be helpful in guiding your independent learning and your use of this book. If you are using this text with others, it might be worthwhile to share your learning expectations together, setting a common direction for your reading, discussion, evaluation, and planning.

This book is so structured that individual chapters can be explored independently or consecutively, depending on your needs and interests. Questions for personal reflection and sharing augment sections highlighting the fundamental concepts of adult life cycle research, adult learning theory, lifelong faith development, and direct implications for leaders and planners of adult religious education. An extensive bibliography concludes the work for those seeking a richer exploration.

CHAPTER I

Do We Really Need Adult Religious Education?

A Tale of the Unknown Adult Religious Education Program

Many parish religious education programs are still heavily focused on the transmission of "sacred information." They often fail to draw adequately from the rich experiences and problem-solving abilities of the adults for whom they are planned. Programs are generally planned during a Monday morning staff meeting over coffee and a Danish. The pastor, associates, and possibly DRE cast lots for the teaching responsibilities according to interest, expertise, and a free evening. Occasionally an outside speaker "who's hot this year" is brought in for variety or because the parish staff has run out of time or steam. Programs are held in the parish school or gym. The mats, nets, balls, trash cans, and bleachers have been shoved into a corner in readiness for the occasion. Events are scheduled on Tuesday, Wednesday, or Thursday evenings and are followed by coffee for those who have time to stay or who want to question the speaker. Announcements are made from the pulpit exhorting the need for this program. Mimeographed flyers are dutifully carried home by the grade school children along with whatever else is left in their Cabbage Patch lunchboxes. The same few parishioners are in attendance, lost amid a sea of folding chairs. The parish staff bemoans the fact of the poor turn-out in the presence of those in attendance, commenting on what a waste of time this has been for the speaker. During a subsequent staff meeting, it is concluded that the parishioners are not interested in adult education! Parish monies are then rightfully channeled into areas that draw the largest numbers—the parish school, children's sports programs, upkeep of the grounds, etc. The parishioners, meanwhile, are wondering why their parish doesn't offer anything in adult education. And the saga continues . . .

QUESTIONS WORTH WRESTLING

1. What are the religious education priorities of our parish? Is adult religious education among them?
2. Is our parish still addressing the "tasks" an adult performs rather than the "person" an adult is?
3. Why is the notion that all Christians are called to ministry largely unknown?
4. Are we using childish methods in attempting to meet adult needs?
5. Is our parish still "telling theological-scriptural-liturgical things" to passive listeners seated in rows of metal folding chairs?
6. Are we still mandating parent sacramental programs?
7. Are we still educating adults in eighth grade classrooms and drafty gyms?
8. Is our parish program in touch with the Church's directives concerning the primacy of adult education?
9. Why are we so fearful of empowering neighborhood clusters and training lay leaders as a means of reaching out to the rest of the parish?
10. Why are we reluctant to develop "family-centered," "life-centered," "problem-centered" programs?
11. Why are we so focused on "content development" rather than on the development of "critically-reflective adults"?

12. Have we failed to realize that adult religious education exists only in relationship to a living liturgy and a Christian community?
13. Are we still supporting "dependent" models of learning for children, youth, and adults?
14. When will we realize that a parish budget is a theological statement?
15. Are parish programs limited to Father's time schedule and expertise?

When Will We Have an Adult Church?

Not too many pastoral leaders would deny that Christianity is a religion for people attaining adulthood both in years and maturity.[1] It is simple to say that Christianity is defined from its adult model. Jesus blessed little children but worked with adults. Unfortunately, it is not as simple finding parish communities where this truth is a reality. Many parishes today are still pouring the bulk of their resources into the pockets of children, hoping that they will hang onto these treasures until they grow up. And that's just what most of us do. We carry around the faith of childhood like a cherished security blanket until it falls apart in our twenties or thirties. Suddenly we are faced with adult-sized problems and a size 6x faith. Most of us are surprised! Some find that their faith is too small and begin searching. They hunt around the nooks and crannies of their parishes for something larger. Some succeed. Many are disappointed. Others choose to stop growing rather than outgrow their faith. About forty percent opt out of the struggle, short-circuiting their faith experiences.

We need parishes with adult-sized models of faith. Our parishes need to assess the resources, ask the questions, and accept the challenges that living in an adult faith community necessitate. The needs and solutions are ours. We are the listeners, mentors, prophets, teachers, community-builders, and healers that can make adult religious education work.

Discerning the Problem

Conflict exists between contemporary principles of adult growth/faith development/learning and the various models of Church operating in our parishes today.[2] Bishops, priests, religious, and laity all find themselves standing along a continuum of philosophical/theological/educational perspectives.[3-5] These positions seem to reflect their personal journeys of human and faith development as well as individual temperament styles.[6-7] Division exists over the extent to which autonomy in believing and moral/ethical decision-making is allowable in our post-conciliar Church. Such autonomy/self-directedness is a hallmark in the process of maturing into adulthood.[8-9]

Various understandings or ways of valuing Church seem to model stages of adulthood. If our particular life or faith stage is reflected in the model we encounter, we feel affirmed in our personhood and in our belief. If not, we feel challenged, threatened, or irritated depending where we are in comparison to that model on the path toward adulthood. This principle seems to hold true for all members in the Church.[10]

Adult religious education offerings in a parish tend to reflect the model of Church held by those who plan them. They reinforce that model in the way that the participants are involved. The participants' expectations and evaluations will in turn tend to reflect their personal models of Church. For this reason, evaluative activities/ instruments act as a challenge for both planners and participants. Each group is called forth to future growth by this creative tension.[11]

The influence of models of Church can also be seen in the understood role of the leader, the methodology used, the climate created, the level of involvement and mutuality encouraged, and the extent to which the learners' experiences and problem-solving abilities are used.[12]

One of the present challenges facing our parishes and their adult religious education programs is the recognition of the influence of personal faith development/models of Church in program planning, climate, methodology, and involvement of the learners. This handicap should be faced squarely. Parishes need to review the norms and guidelines of the Church regarding adult religious education as well as continue to grow in their awareness of the implications of adult life cycle, faith development, and learning characteristics research. All aspects of parish adult education need to be reviewed regularly in this regard. Adult educators need to evaluate the understanding they have of their role in relation to those with whom they learn. Budgets need to be channeled to reflect the Church's priority in adult religious education.

Risking a Vision

The primary purpose of a parish faith community is to meet the religious needs of its members. Parishes exist to promote faith in individuals and in communities. Local parishes are charged with the task of giving their members a sense of purpose, an opportunity for Christian identity, an impetus for growth and maturation, models of support, consolation and reconciliation, examples of the Christian search for meaning, a visible expression of norms and values, and a visible challenge as prophet in the world. Apart from this mission, parishes remain communities of children. As such, they will be unable to provide an environment in which the religious understanding of the next generation can develop to an adult level. In many parishes, the goal of an adult Church is a vision that no one is asked to make real.[13]

Parishes need to make use of research on adult development and psychology, principles of needs assessment and program design, and characteristics and styles of adult learning. They should take the directives of the Church on adult religious education more seriously.

While aiming to enrich the faith life of individuals at their particular stages of development, every form of catechesis is oriented in some way to the catechesis of adults. (NCD #32)

The primary reason for adult catechesis—its first and essential objective—is to help adults themselves grow to maturity of faith as members of the Church and society. (NCD #40)

The act of faith is a free response to God's grace; and maximum human freedom comes with the self-possession and responsibility of adulthood. This is one of the principal reasons for regarding adult catechesis as the chief form of catechesis. To assign primacy to adult catechesis does not mean sacrificing catechesis at other age levels; it means making sure that what is done earlier is carried to its culmination in adulthood. (NCD #188)

Because of its importance and because all other forms of catechesis are oriented in some way to it, catechesis of adults must have priority at all levels of the Church. (NCD #188)

Through a parish catechetical board, a committee, or a chairperson of adult catechesis, the pastor should see to it that catechetical programs are available for adults as part of the total catechetical program. Parish planning groups should be creative in designing ways to reach and motivate adults to participate. (NCD #225)

Catechesis for adults respects and makes use of their experiences . . . their personal skills, and other resources they bring to catechetical programs; whenever possible, adults should teach and learn from one another. Much effective learning comes from reflecting upon one's experiences in the light of faith. Adults must be helped to translate such reflection into practical steps to meet their responsibilities in a Christian manner. . . . This suggests the use of discussion techniques . . . other methods, in fact, all methods available to sound secular education. (NCD #185)

Adults should play a central role in their own education. They should identify their needs, plan ways to meet them, and take part in the evaluation of programs and activities. (NCD #185)

The total learning environment of the parish is an important factor in motivating adults. Programs for adults should offer positive reinforcements and rewards . . . adults should be encouraged to realize their potential for becoming religiously mature—or more mature persons. (NCD #189)

[**Paragraphs Quoted Directly From:** United States Catholic Conference, *Sharing the Light of Faith: National Catechetical Directory for Catholics in the United States* (Washington, D.C.: Department of Education, United States Catholic Conference, 1979), pp. 18, 21, 111–113, 138–139.]

Basic Premises of Adult Education

◇ Co-equality of learning is a fundamental disposition in adult education.

◇ Networking within adult systems affects both learner and leader and impacts on retention of what is learned.

◇ All four learning styles should be represented in a balanced adult education program.

◇ Every parish and group must determine what their commitment to adult learning is before program planning begins. Budgets, personnel and resource availability are key factors in that determination.

◇ Creating conflicts, resolving conflicts and learning contradictions are positive aspects of adult situations.

◇ Identification of the learning needs of the group or parish is a key element in the initial planning process.

◇ Identify the structures which support or suppress the intended efforts for adult educational programming.

◇ Hospitality and a sense of parish ownership are important felt needs. "My goodness, they'll be going to each other for help!" is a sentiment that reveals the resistance to empowerment that can short-circuit adult learning.

◇ The individual and the institutional Church must both undergo a religious process of growth. Measuring that growth is objective as well as subjective. Use tools of evaluation liberally. They enable future planning to be meaningful and effective.

◇ Lifelong learning is the keystone to adult education. It is a process and not a program. Programs are part of the process.

◇ Relational dimensions in adult learning situations are very important. People engaged in adult learning situations must feel relaxation, a sense of accomplishment and ownership of their own learning experiences.

CHAPTER II

Exploring Christian Adulthood

It Isn't Anything Like the Way I Thought It Would Be

From infancy, we followed the dangling carrot of adulthood. Physical growth, education, and psychological development were all seen as avenues to that great day when we would all be grown-up. Relatives asked, "What are you going to be when you grow up?" Parents challenged, "When are you going to grow up?" Teachers exhorted, "Don't you know that you'll need these skills when you grow up?"

It wasn't long before we discovered that being all grown-up carried with it certain powers and privileges. Grown-ups were free to leave the protective family unit, to vote, to drive, to drink, to make legal transactions, to participate in all forms of entertainment, to determine their use of time and money, to choose or refuse schooling, and to shape their own life-styles. We eagerly awaited the day of our independence, a time when we too would be free from the burden of growth. We longed for our great day of "having it all together." We approached adulthood with great expectations, anticipating a life of stability, maturity, and settling down as finished persons.[1]

Actual adulthood has taken most of us by surprise. The real experiences of adult living are often different from the myths we've spun in our earlier years. Instead of feeling settled down, we are swamped with times of uprootedness. Rather than seeing ourselves as "all grown-up," we feel the need to grow. For most of us, the realization that adulthood is a time of continuous change came as a startling blow. The real demands of everyday living have outgrown most of our assumptions. We find ourselves faced with a challenging journey continuously outgrowing all that we have to accomplish it.[2]

The central challenge of adult life concerns our understanding of and response to change. Adulthood is a process of on-going growth.[3] Adults grow in and out of struggle, in and out of questions, and in and out of crises. Rather than being all together, there are times when we feel that we are losing our grip, falling apart, having a breakdown, or experiencing mental problems, when, in fact, what we are really experiencing are moments of growth announced by the painful feeling of needing to change.[4]

No One Ever Told Us

Rather than being an attainable condition, adulthood is really a psychological ideal toward which we are challenged to strive. No one is ever fully an adult. Adulthood is a developmental ideal involving all that we are physically, intellectually, emotionally, morally, socially, and religiously. It is an invitation involving the integration of opposites, a deepening of interdependence, and an openness toward wholeness involving self-emptying for others.[5] As in childhood and adolescence, adulthood involves a movement through relatively predictable steps or stages toward greater complexity, competence, and integration.[6] Adults, too, must learn to relate to their new selves every step along the way. The tragedy is that most adults keep this realization neatly tucked away, reinforcing the myths of adulthood for themselves while passing them on to the next generation. Surrounded by these myths, each of us thinks that we are somehow the only exception. We inhibit the creativity of our responses and fail to become a source of wisdom for one another. The gift of our unique themes and variations throughout the adult life cycle is lost as a heritage for future generations.

7

Why Haven't We Been Told?

Only within the last two decades have researchers studied the developmental patterns and insights within the 20–70 year-old bracket. There is a great deal of material on the development of children and adolescents ages 0–10 and 10–20. A growing body of research on gerontology picks up again at age 75. The changes in both these populations are more dramatic. The physical, emotional, intellectual, and social changes in the young and very old are noticeable. The developmental changes of adults moving through their 20's, 30's, 40's, 50's, 60's, and 70's are more subtle.[7]

What Have Researchers Discovered?

◇ The adult life cycle refers to the changing patterns of needs, interests, and responses which occur in adulthood from the transition out of adolescence through mid-life and older adulthood to death.[8]

◇ To call change in these patterns "development" is to suggest that the later stages of the process depend upon, include, and in some sense bring to fulfillment/completion what has gone on before. This movement is more accurately thought of as a circular progression rather than a linear achievement.[9]

◇ Development in the adult life cycle can be understood as a movement toward greater complexity, competence, and integration involving all the capacities of the human person.[10]

◇ Development in adult life is the result of growthful responses to crises and support experienced in the context of daily living. The thoughts, feelings, hopes, values, dreams, choices, abilities, and behaviors of adults in interaction with their social settings are all subject to psychosocial development.[11]

◇ Adult development occurs in loosely sequenced, predictable stages, through which persons journey in fluid movement. The journey is gradual, continuous, and multidimensional. It is punctuated with spurts, setbacks, and plateaus.[12–14]

◇ Not everyone develops at the same pace or in the same way. There are individual themes and variations. Adults are similar in their development and yet always unique. We cannot pigeonhole ourselves or others in rigid categories.

◇ Something happens cognitively, emotionally, and volitionally as a person matures, creating greater potential over time to reach higher stages of development. It is important that we do not apply a capitalistic bias, comparing our growth and the growth of others in terms of achievement and upward mobility. Adult maturity is not a matter of competition.[15]

◇ Adult development is age-related, but not age-specific. Although adults in our culture tend to experience life changes/events at certain times in their lives, significant variations do occur. Individuals do not necessarily proceed successfully through all stages. Some stay at intermediate stages. Some regress. Others advance faster. Each adult brings along a unique history in wrestling transitions. No two transitions are absolutely identical in onset, timing, duration, source, effect, and degree of stress. A great deal depends upon the resources and support available to those attempting to negotiate change.[16–18]

◇ Developmental stages that are ignored or unsuccessfully tackled will resurface until negotiated successfully. The unfinished business of early years will continue to demand attention in later stages of life.[19–20]

◇ At each stage there are certain kinds of growing to be done, knowledge and skills to be acquired, and psychological accomplishments to be achieved. There are certain developmental tasks that need to be learned and adaptations that need to be made in order to adjust and change in response to life's demands.[21–23]

◇ Passing from one stage to another constitutes a significant transition. Adults lose equilibrium in earlier stages and must regain it in later stages. Their current skills no longer enable them to meet the demands of their current experiences. They must disengage themselves of their current status, painfully float in mid-air, attempt new ideas or behaviors, and then re-engage themselves with new coping skills and resources.[24–26]

◇ Adults experience transitions as posing challenges, creating stress, and offering opportunities for growth. The amount of emotional crisis experienced varies among individuals. Everyone does not have to undergo every

8

condition that can be encountered in a transition. But everyone undergoes a unique developmental process involving questioning, letting go, and changing. Individuals do not handle each crisis in the same way and with the same intensity. A great deal depends upon current coping skills and available resources, challenges, and support.[27-28]

◇ Specific life events, whether internal or external, often signal the beginning or end of life stages, although significant events occur within as well as between stages.[29]

◇ Most researchers see events as having a precipitating rather than causative effect, often releasing latent needs still having potential for action. Due to this phenomenon, transitions overlap, connect, and interpenetrate, while the current transition is predominant.[30]

◇ Human development occurs in the context of human systems which challenge and support growth. Personal settings and the network of personal, institutional, and cultural settings all have a major effect on human development. Human systems and personal settings are the places where personal development occurs.[31]

◇ Human development is culturally relative. Development is what a particular culture or subculture says it is.[32]

What the research on development in the adult life cycle can offer us lies mainly in generalizations about ourselves and others as we move through time and experiences. These insights should never take the place of first-hand knowledge and direct contact. Many people do not fit into the generalizations of the social sciences, no matter how subtle the gradation.

SOME QUESTIONS FOR REFLECTION AND SHARING

1. What were the myths, ideals, and expectations that you carried from childhood and adolescence into adult life?
   Where did they originate?

2. How has your understanding of adulthood changed?
   What factors have influenced your present understanding?
   What does adulthood mean to you at this time in your life?
   Do you think your definition of adulthood will change in the future?
   Explain.

3. What are the ways in which you communicate your current understanding of adulthood to children? youth? other adults?
   Should this be a consideration?

4. What cultural definitions of adulthood are you aware of?
   How do these affirm or differ from yours?

5. List the main planned and unplanned events in your life thus far.
   How have these events affected your physical, intellectual, emotional, social, moral, and religious development?

6. List the major transitions/crises with which you have already wrestled.
   What was it like to grow through each one of these transitions/crises?
   Did you react to and handle each one in the same way?
   Did they all have the same impact on your life?

7. Reflect back on your answers and on the answers of those who have shared with you.
   What conclusions can be drawn about the adult life cycle from your experience?

Adulthood: A Changing Portrait

In this section of descriptions, it may be helpful to imagine each section as a school of artistic endeavor. While running the risk of oversimplification, and giving an incomplete comparison, it still serves the purpose of creating an imagery that may well "speak louder than words." Each transition of adulthood may be likened

9

to the work of a particular school of art or master. They are portraits colored by their own rich treasury of experience, vision, and performance. Each brush stroke of time lends completion to the total effort of a lifetime. While no one period is exclusively self-defining, each helps to create the overall rich portrait of a life. There are certain tasks, characteristics, and expectations associated with every transition period of adulthood. These are generalizations of a society, and individuals will vary in degree of their own experience just as individual artists of a period vary in their works. No two masters use the palette in the same way.

The Age Twenty Transition
(approximately 17 to 22–24)

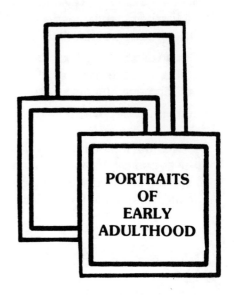

In any impressionistic painting, one notes the mosaic-like composition which culminates in a total effect of a united whole. The various strokes of the brush, while varied and deliberately non-formative, contribute to a total picture that reflects the overall clear and concise image. The period of transition which spans the ages 17 to 24 is one which is rich in the formative impressions. It is much like the paintings of that period with brush strokes from childhood and early adolescence blending against a background of relational learning and independence. It is a time for creating the dream and hoping toward an adulthood of fulfillment. This period, more than any other, is a time for testing the total effect against the parts of which it is made. Intimate relationships are being explored, mentors are being sought, time is seemingly endless, and the pursuit of a social life is highly active. This is a time for looking at the parts and not giving a high regard to the integration of the parts to the whole.

Key Concerns:[33]

1. Establishment of independence from parents by assuming responsibility and growing in self-awareness
2. Formation of a tentative self-identity as an adult in the world
3. Creation of a dream expressing all that is hoped for in the adult world and the goals needed to realize that dream
4. Searching for a mentor who will foster the dream and assist in shaping the developing personality and ego ideals

General Characteristics:[34]

1. Peak physical condition
2. Great mental and physical power compared to small responsibility load
3. Exploring intimate relationships, getting lost in physical contact and the resultant feelings; becoming more comfortable with intimacy and thus growing in responsiveness to others
4. Time is perceived as endless; options limitless; death is a distant abstraction
5. Marriage is at this time modeled after parent-child relationship, each spouse parenting the other
6. Occupation and/or family choices related to the dream; decisions are generally made without adequate information
7. Change is seen as a thrill and adventure
8. Very active social life

The Twenties
(approximately 23 to 28)

The period of the twenties, characterized by physical and mental prowess, is much like the Van Gogh era of intensity marked with determination. It is reflective of the time when strong illusionary elements are forming the maturing adult. There is a preoccupation with the present and a desire to integrate the self with another. The boldness of color and intensity of statement found in the work of Van Gogh can give a rich imagery to this period of transition toward adulthood. Persons in their mid to late twenties are beginning new adventures and trying out their life dreams on the canvas of their prior experiences in family and career relationships. Theirs is a portrait of self-actualization and illusionary planning.

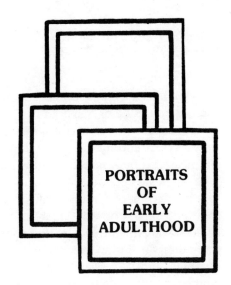

PORTRAITS OF EARLY ADULTHOOD

Key Concerns:[35]
1. To bring to culmination and self-realization the identity tentatively established during the Age Twenty Transition
2. To integrate the self with another
3. The dream creates the "one true course"
4. Fulfilling the dream and living one's identity in loving and working

General Characteristics:[36]
1. Unsure of whether they are a boy-man or a girl-woman
2. Skill and coordination are at their prime
3. Mental abilities good
4. Emotions are modulated, trying to "behave as adults should"
5. Still separating from parents, beginnings of a new relationship with them
6. Greatest variety in social activities
7. Dream still has a strong illusionary component: denial of one's death, belief that one is independent of others, thinking that one can achieve or fulfill a career without self-knowledge, time has limitless possibilities
8. Time—the present is better than the past, the future is positive and awaited eagerly
9. Power is still great—load is increasing
10. Possible parenting, family obligations become stressors

The Age Thirty Transition
(approximately 28 to 33–35)

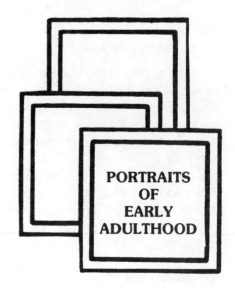

PORTRAITS OF EARLY ADULTHOOD

The modern school of painting subscribes to interpretation of emotion through shape and color. A look at the masters of this period, such as Paul Klee or Salvador Dali, give us a glimpse into struggles for human expression. In many ways a parallel can be made between this school of art and the transition into the thirties. This period of time is characterized by a search for how the self penetrates the world. It is a time when life becomes real and the search for the inhibited self begins to emerge. Persons in this group begin the process of examining their roles and setting new life goals for themselves. Parts of the whole are seen clearly and graphically. Just as the artist's intent is more of a statement than an illusion, persons in this period of life transitions are more assertive and self-reliant. Theirs is a portrait of contradictions, role changes, and emerging interdependence. Like the pieces of mastery from the brush of the cubic artists, persons in their early thirties are caught in the expression of their adult role, their changing life styles, and their emerging power.

Key Concerns:[37]

1. To search for the self and the way the self penetrates the world
   ◊ a time of questioning; strong self-centeredness
   ◊ life as an adult becomes real
   ◊ time begins to become more permanent
   ◊ searching for the parts of the self that have been inhibited
   ◊ males become restless and begin to re-evaluate career component; set new goals
   ◊ females experience a time of upheaval and restlessness, investigating both identity and role options; emerging of independent dream if married
   ◊ single people see time swiftly passing and the question of marriage and childbearing becomes a pressing one; commitment and goals to a vocation
   ◊ married people are both wrapped up in self and deny the other the right to be selfish

General Characteristics:[38]

1. Physical and mental abilities are still in their prime
2. Responsibilities are creating more load to power; less free time for new pursuits
3. No longer as much need to prove self to parents; parts of self that are like parents begin to be realized and accepted; authority with males and their fathers becomes great
4. Children begin to replace parents as center for concern
5. Decreased interest in social activities; self-reliance and independence
6. Women are at their sexual fullest between thirty and forty; men are beginning to lose their capacity for multiple orgasms; sexual relations are better than in the twenties because of better communication and experience
7. Males continue to be assertive and task-oriented rule followers
   Females continue to be nurturing and are more emotionally complex than males at this age
8. Family life is the major stressor
9. Adults are taking their first steps toward interdependence and mutuality as they recognize the need for dependence and independence

Primary Life Tasks of Early Adulthood[39]
(indicative but not exclusive)

Vocation and Career

Exploring career options
Choosing a career line
Getting a job
Being interviewed
Learning job skills
Getting along at work
Getting ahead at work
Getting job protection
Dealing with the issue of military service
Changing jobs

Enjoyment of Leisure

Choosing new hobbies
Finding new friends
Joining organizations
Planning your time
Buying equipment
Planning family recreation
Leading recreational activities

Health

Keeping fit
Planning diets
Finding and using health services
Preventing accidents
Using first aid
Understanding children's diseases
Understanding how the human body functions
Buying and using drugs and medicine
Developing a healthy life style
Recognizing the symptoms of physical and
    mental illness

Community Living

Relating to school and teachers
Learning about community resources
Learning how to get help
Preparing to vote
Developing leadership skills
Keeping up with the world
Taking action in the community
Organizing community activities for children and
    youth

Home and Family Living

Courting
Selecting a mate
Preparing for marriage
Family planning
Preparing for children
Raising children
Understanding children
Preparing children for school
Helping children in school
Solving marital problems
Using family counseling
Managing a home
Financial planning
Managing money
Buying goods and services
Making home repairs
Gardening

Personal Development

Improving your reading ability
Improving your writing ability
Improving your speaking ability
Improving your listening ability
Continuing your general education
Developing your religious faith
Improving problem-solving skills
Making better decisions
Getting along with people
Understanding yourself
Finding your self-identity
Discovering your aptitudes
Clarifying your values
Understanding other people
Learning to be self-directing
Improving personal appearance
Establishing intimate relations
Dealing with conflict
Making use of personal counseling

Taken From: Malcolm S. Knowles. *The Modern Practice of Adult Education: From Pedagogy to Andragogy*, rev. ed. (Chicago: Follett Publishing Company, 1980), pp. 263–264 (minor adjustments have been made).

The Thirties
(approximately 33–35 to 40)

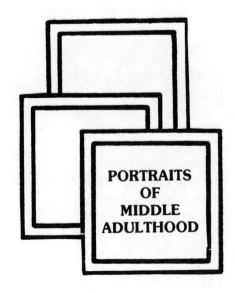

PORTRAITS OF MIDDLE ADULTHOOD

The quest for stability asserts itself strongly during this stage of adult development.

Adults in this period speak of their goals as tasks and not dreams. They paint clearly the picture of their values and recognize the limitations, both physically and mentally, that are approaching. In the realistic landscapes and madonna-like women of the Dutch and French masters, there is an attention to detail that makes of the canvas a photograph. The need in these works is not so much one of expressing the line and shape of things, as it is a matter of recreating the experience of the moment. It is an attempt to hold on to the time and place, just as persons of this period of adulthood are holding fast to the strong family ties, coping with feelings of emptiness and changed role expectations. Men are growing more doubtful of their pursuits and women are questioning their relationship to spouse and family. There is clearly less self-contentment in both sexes during this time of transition.

Key Concerns:[40]
1. To advance and maintain stability without too much accommodation
   ◊ to strive to advance on one's psychosocial ladder accompanied by the desire for stability within marriage/relationships with significant other, family
   ◊ marital difficulties are covered over; accommodation occurs
2. De-illusionment—to remove from the dream the illusionary elements
   ◊ peaking of early adulthood aspirations
   ◊ "So what!" "Is this all there is?" "There is no there, there!"
   ◊ doubts and fears of twenties and thirties are still there despite personal achievement and success
   ◊ feelings of emptiness
3. Sense that time is limited affects priorities
   ◊ need to be established according to values; with a limitation of priorities comes self-awareness
   ◊ new decisions on how one will spend time
4. Authority-Mutuality: to achieve authority with mutuality
   ◊ when to be dependent, when to be authoritative, when to be interdependent

General Characteristics:[41]
1. People pass their physical prime around age thirty-five, but changes are slow and some people do not notice until their forties
2. Mental abilities are still keen
3. Load begins to increase with power
4. Strong family priority begins to emerge for males; career-family duality begins
5. Women now dream of self and others; duality not faced at this time
6. Males become more interdependent within the family unit; females explore diverse options
7. To avoid conflict each spouse covers over difficulties
8. Marriage is affected by de-illusionment; partners begin blaming each other for their felt sense of emptiness and for not fulfilling their illusions
9. Males begin to feel a duality between career-family and the self
10. Adults begin to feel that they are part of the older generation as their parents grow older and their children are noticeably growing up
11. Priorities for family life are noted in social life
12. Men follow the more refined dream of their twenties while women establish their new dream

13. Adults now speak of their goals as tasks, not as wishes and needs
14. Adults find action more important than faith and ideals
15. By the end of this period men are full of doubts and anxiety; women are asking questions about the fit of their life structure
    ◊ women ask from the view of changing their "self"
    ◊ men find that their denial has not worked and are thrown into emotional turmoil
16. Men in their forties have less sense of contentment and self-direction than women; most men's mid-life awaits them in their forties since up until now they only make small adjustments in their careers

Age Forty Transition
(approximately 40 to 45–50)

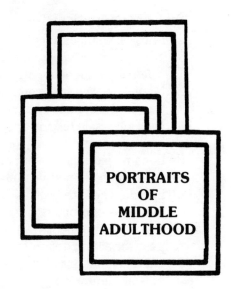

One need only look to the works of Rembrandt or Monet to see the effect of discipline, experience, and creativity. Their paintings depict the relinquishment of self-deception and illusion found in other periods of art. Just like the transition and passage from ages 40–45, there is a sense of satisfaction and completeness to their efforts.

Part of the joy of this period of life is the greater certainty of values, concerns, goals, and moral and ethical beliefs. This period, more than any other, is one of authenticity. Men and women perceive their lives against a framework of a greater reality and time becomes finite. While still striving to express their individuality, both men and women in this age group develop a stronger sense of interdependence and mutuality. There is a strong sense of inter-generational thinking among this age group. Men and women often become mentors to others and give up some of their earlier role models and mentors. Personalities become well situated and maturity characterizes activity. The portrait of a person in his/her late forties is one akin to that of the masters.

Key Concerns:[42]
1. De-illusionment continues; relinquishment of self-deceptions
   ◊ family, work, and health become real stressors
   ◊ the dream is perceived as less absolute, success is less essential, failure is less devastating
   ◊ satisfaction with what is and making that better
   ◊ looking for quality in work; intrinsic value and meaning
   ◊ women launching independent dreams
   ◊ men formulating interdependent dreams
2. Individuation—introspection into the gaps between reality and goals
   ◊ giving vent to neglected parts of self
   ◊ new realities of adjusted dream expand sense of self
   ◊ greater certainty in values, goals, concerns, moral and ethical beliefs
   ◊ old situations have new meaning
   ◊ less "oughts and shoulds," more wants
   ◊ becoming authentic, dropping masks, role-playing, status symbols
   ◊ attracted to authentic peers
3. Establishment of modified identity
   ◊ clarify place in the world resulting from re-evaluation
   ◊ wrestling with inner dualities; real vs. ideal, young vs. old, mortality vs. immortality, destructive vs. creative, male vs. female, being separate vs. being attached, generativity vs. self-absorption
4. Time is perceived as finite, fleeting; amount left to live
   ◊ living in the present; fear of future
5. Career questions in terms of goals, values, priorities, concerns for future

15

◇ "I have gone as far as I can"; thoughts of retirement begin

6. Marriage—autonomy vs. mutuality; rollercoaster of feelings stemming from insecurity, vulnerability, questioning; growth toward interdependence
7. Children—responsibility of setting standards; feeling pleasure or jealousy at their progress
    ◇ feeling part of the older generation as they grow up
    ◇ begin to verbalize regrets in childbearing; begin to accept negative/destructive qualities in their parenting
    ◇ emptying nest creates role confusion; invites deepening of spousal relationship

General Characteristics:[43]

1. Physical changes announcing the loss of youth
    ◇ males fear loss of sexual prowess
    ◇ females experience increased sexual desire and assertiveness
2. Mental abilities still prime; dealing more effectively with increased load
3. Fear of death fosters attitudes and behaviors of denial
4. New interest in religion and philosophy to increase power and cope with increasing financial, life, and health concerns
5. Become parents to their parents as they increase in dependency
    ◇ beginning to resolve authority issue with parents
6. Interdependence begins—cooperation, willingness to listen increases, trying to understand the views of spouse and others
7. Males give up mentors and become good mentors expressing generativity
8. Less socializing; return to family interest in friends the "couple" shares
9. Interpersonal relationships—males develop competence and assertiveness; females interested in altruism, nurturance, generativity
    ◇ spouse becomes "best friend"
    ◇ friends chosen from other places than work for males; women still relate to fellow workers as recreational partners
10. Leisure activities foster creativity, happiness, self-respect
    ◇ more family activities; less going out
    ◇ singles are invited less than other couples and may feel lonely
11. No longer necessary to prove self to parents/others; personality is well-situated
    ◇ *males* emphasize interpersonal-aggressive over aggressive-achievement; wide swing in behavior as testing out roles; more nurturant and generative than before; feelings surface; desire for both love and work
    ◇ males tend to be more passive when philosophical issues are at stake yet are active when achievement is questioned; not afraid of power struggle
    ◇ stress leads to anger
    ◇ trying to integrate emotional selves
    ◇ *females* are driven by social-service values
    ◇ speak of ease and contentment; confident and accepting
    ◇ more aggressive and action-oriented expanding from domesticity into a broader work environment if married
    ◇ sense of freedom as nest empties
    ◇ less emotional conflict than men at this stage; they are more self-aware and can effectively manipulate their environment in a competent, confident, generative, mutual way

Late Middle Adulthood
(approximately 45–47 to 50)

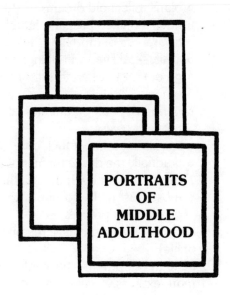

PORTRAITS
OF
MIDDLE
ADULTHOOD

The period from the late forties to the early fifties is one of integrated satisfaction. There are new tasks to perform and a sense of satisfaction with the earlier phases of one's life. Views tend to be more conservative and while physical limitations begin to assert themselves, career expectations are at their peak. Adults care for their aging parents. Plans are made for retirement and dreams of the future are in better perspective. Like the work of El Greco, the highlights of one's life are the emphasis of the portrait. The work of this master is easily recognized by the extended figures often highlighted with bright accent lines. A review of life is in order at this transition point. The highlights of career, family life, financial and social acceptability, moral and ethical reputation are but a few of the accents of this period. Against a backdrop of increased leisure, marital satisfaction, and career achievements, persons in this phase are clearly identifiable by their portrait of genuineness.

Key Concerns:[44]
1. Stability and satisfaction
   ◊ opportunity to live out and act upon the changes in the self that have been made
   ◊ sense of quietude; men more peaceful than women
   ◊ each individual has a newly integrated structure; the task is to regain equilibrium; to live out of the new format
   ◊ conservative and moralistic view of life; feeling that things are good enough, successful enough, rich enough
2. Mellowness as a result of the satisfaction affecting all aspects of life; sense of peacefulness with self and others

General Characteristics:[45]
1. Physical aches, pains, and signs of aging continue; change of life begins
2. Mental tasks take longer but are still done well; load lessens but power is still high
3. Marital satisfaction is high and remains that way through the fifties
   ◊ each looks at the other with sympathy and affection, is autonomous and has integrated male/female qualities
   ◊ true love is the consequence of previous years of growing; a love that permits the other to grow regardless of personal gain
   ◊ spouse as "social companion"
   ◊ singles move to first marriage/remarriage considerations; those who remain single deepen vocational commitment and seek out significant others
   ◊ tendency to dwell on the good that has happened to their children rather than the problems
   ◊ women transfer offspring nurturance to career/consolidating their environment (fixing up the home, gardening, refurbishing wardrobe, etc.)
4. Adults care for aging parents
5. Males begin to give credit to mentors/maternal relatives for their influence
   Females still have a mentor or are in the throes of giving one up
   Both are ripe to mentor younger adults; generativity grows in such a relationship
6. Career—males begin to express more concerns about sharing than achievement; they assume a nurturing role at work, supporting peers; talk of retirement increases
7. Time—resignation to the finitude of time; acceptance of restricted scope on future activities; planning the possible for the future

     ◇ plans reflect old dreams

     ◇ have a unified past and future, living in the present with previously set priorities

     ◇ awareness of mortality, "Do it now!"; mortality and time perceptions closely linked

8. Socially—satisfied with things as they are

     ◇ go out more often to satisfy desires for food, contact with others, interests, aesthetic delight, help others

     ◇ period of peak organizational involvement for men; enter activities for their own sake and not to prove prowess

     ◇ socializing to meet their own needs

     ◇ gradually the desire for friends, to be active and involved, slows, but would feel lost without friends; close network even though they do not see each other often

     ◇ most reasons to go out of the house by the end of this period revolve around helping others; generativity prevails

9. Leisure—major pursuits: reading, discussion, religion, helping others (remain important for the rest of life)

10. Male development—have integrated autonomy and dependence thus becoming more affectionate, more expressive, less aggressive

     ◇ power equals load; no longer enhances the ego; interests in community and true generativity

     ◇ feelings of inner peace; desire for religion

11. Female development—desire to do something worthwhile than to get ahead

     ◇ look for activities that bring meaning to life (political, aesthetic, religious)

     ◇ are satisfied, stable, assertive, unique persons

12. Overall characteristics—genuine, tend to exercise good judgment, to cooperate, to be dependable, responsible, steady, share joy, fear, guilt, love, and sorrow for others

     ◇ no longer wear masks/play roles

     ◇ use altruism and suppression as defense mechanisms instead of fantasy, projection and reaction formation

     ◇ rather than create a scene or blame others, these adults feel it isn't worth it, life's too short, best forgotten

     ◇ the result is a genuinely sympathetic, giving, productive, dependable person

Primary Life Tasks of Middle Adulthood[46]
(indicative but not exclusive)

Vocation and Career

Learning advanced job skills
Supervising others
Changing careers
Dealing with unemployment
Planning for retirement
Making second careers for mothers

Enjoyment of Leisure

Finding less active hobbies
Broadening your cultural interests
Learning new recreational skills
Finding new friends
Joining new organizations
Planning recreation for two

Health

Adjusting to physiological changes
Changing diets
Controlling weight
Getting exercise
Having annual medical exam
Compensating for losses in strength

Community Living

Taking more social responsibility
Taking leadership roles in organizations
Working for the welfare of others
Engaging in politics
Organizing community improvement activities

Home and Family Living

Helping teenage children to become adults
Letting your children go
Relating to one's spouse as a person
Adjusting to aging parents
Learning to cook for two
Planning for retirement

Personal Development

Finding new interests
Keeping out of a rut
Compensation for physiological changes
Dealing with change
Developing emotional flexibility
Learning to cope with crises
Developing a realistic time perspective

Taken From: Malcolm S. Knowles, *The Modern Practice of Adult Education: From Pedagogy to Andragogy*, rev. ed. (Chicago: Follett Publishing Company, 1980), pp. 263–264.

The Fifties
(approximately 50 to 60)

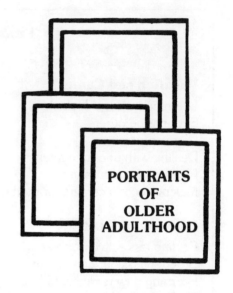

PORTRAITS OF OLDER ADULTHOOD

The period of the late fifties into the early sixties is one of conservative and practical leadership. This is a time for accepting limitations, both in the world and within oneself. It is a time for accepting a certain lack of control over the complexities of a new world. These persons are the leaders and the decision-makers, but they personally cope with increased self-doubt about their future, their family, and their society. They are persons faced with the reality of decreased physical and mental abilities. The artists of the early Egyptian period were preoccupied with showing both arms and legs in their frontal paintings. The Egyptians wanted to express the wholeness of their subjects. Their attention to detail was painstakingly etched in stone. Like frescoes and other works done against stone, theirs was a labor of magnificence done against an unyielding surface. While persons in this period of transition cannot change the past and are forced to accept the unyielding character of their own personal histories, they do have the promise of fulfillment as mentors for others. They have the opportunity to show their wholeness and share their experiences with the greater and extended family. Their limitations are measured against the depth and richness of their experiences. Activities reflect their self-concept, and persons during this transition are challenged by the task to remain flexible and retool their interests.

Key Concerns:[47]

1. Mellowness—feeling comfortable about oneself
   ◊ perceive selves as mature, able to deal with life
   ◊ strength is found in religion and philosophy
   ◊ life brings high satisfaction; "I am in my prime!"
   ◊ these persons are looked to for leadership which enhances feelings of self-esteem; they are the norm-setters, the decision-makers
   ◊ at peak of creativity and productivity bringing self-satisfaction and tolerance for others
   ◊ they support the system, are honest, of stable temperament, but encourage debate while calming others
2. Integrity and generativity—integration of the two brings wisdom and caring
   ◊ by age sixty, adults begin to have a diminished self-concept, exhibiting traits such as calmness, conservatism, practicality, slowness, thoughtfulness, absentmindedness, and diverse disinterestedness
   ◊ patience increases as they realize that things take time
   ◊ values may change; the world perceived by those in their sixties is dangerous and complex; something that one conforms to and does not reform
   ◊ realization of lack of control may be devastating; one cannot reform what one no longer understands or is involved in
   ◊ possibility for serious health concerns, "I can't do all the things I used to do"; illness may occur
   ◊ may devise protective coping mechanisms
   ◊ the task is to be able to replace the physical with an unshakable sense of personal worth
   ◊ when ability is combined with past experiences these people lead with wisdom
   ◊ integrity is the acceptance that this life is the only one and must be lived at its best
   ◊ generativity leads to care for all humanity
   ◊ integrated together, they yield wisdom shared with others; tranquility ensues
3. Regret vs. acceptance—the realization that one cannot push personal values and cultural beliefs on others
   ◊ the control of society is slipping away

    ◊ new opportunities to learn from the next generation

    ◊ adults who regret and accept have the flexibility needed to use wisdom effectively

  4. Life review—death is accepted as a new presence

    ◊ questioning of mortality in terms of life's meaning

    ◊ review of their contribution to the world; validation of identity

    ◊ clearer picture of one's life emerges; helps to mitigate fears

    ◊ often involves an evaluation of a big event in one's past

General Characteristics:[48]

1. Aging process continues; ability to compensate for physical losses
2. Mental ability still acute; takes longer to learn some material; load is less while power is still quite high
3. Time—is NOW; the present is prime; little concern for past or future

    ◊ more life lies behind than ahead; past and present satisfying

    ◊ past and future are rarely mentioned together

    ◊ more satisfied with things the way they are now; approve of things that earlier in life they would not have condoned

4. Marriage—reflects mellowness of the period; satisfaction high

    ◊ spouse as "valued companion" and source of support; worries about the death of spouse more than his/her own

    ◊ spouses want approval from each other; co-equals; autonomy; mutuality

    ◊ less responsible for children; want their approval

    ◊ grandparenting may begin

    ◊ women make the decisions and men are more passive; peak wife dominance (hormonal shift and neglected self emerges)

    ◊ growth potential for sexual relationship if both have resolved their change of life

5. Parents—their parents are no longer perceived as the cause of personal problems; this realization comes with feelings of guilt for past problems with parents

    ◊ parents are aging more and need more care/last parent has died catapulting them into the senior generation

6. Social—emphasis is on sharing joy and sorrow rather than glamor and power

    ◊ moments of deep feeling are cherished

    ◊ friends are highly valued, especially as some die; not replaced

    ◊ emotional topics like sex and health are avoided

    ◊ organizational involvement is at peak during mid-fifties for women

7. Leisure—people in their fifties want leisure NOW; do what they always wanted to do

    ◊ free time is for personal enjoyment; tempo of life has slowed

8. Occupation—not prime focus; little career change; make fewer demands

    ◊ retirement and financial security are major concerns

    ◊ more concerned about sharing than achievement

    ◊ women have more roles than men; men are more concerned about health and their bodies than women

    ◊ women use age concealment to keep job; remain in sports; can act out of comfortable modes of behavior (impulsive, aggressive, egocentric) as a form of denial

    ◊ males are less confident and have fewer life satisfactions by sixty; women are less threatened

Sixty Plus
(through the senior years)

It might be irreverent to suggest that this period of transition is most often associated with the portrait of "Whistler's Mother." The passive rocking chair image of senior living is too often the mind-set of senior citizens. In a modern society of innovative ideas and opportunities for seniors, it would be a grave disservice to portray senior living in this fashion. While admittedly the physical and mental powers of individuals in their sixties, seventies, and eighties may not be as agile as they once were, there is an unlimited wealth of experience, integrity, and self-expression to share. This is a phase of interdependent living characterized by life reviews and a sense of satisfaction, but it is also a time for greater leisure pursuits and new interests. It is a period much like the American school of art which produced the James Whistlers and others. Theirs is a rugged determination, a sense of austerity, and straightforwardness. This period can be the most self-satisfying one in terms of human development. Stress factors of a different nature must be dealt with and new expectations of self must be formed. Keeping interested in a new world and learning to live alone can bring anxiety, but they can also bring new opportunities for self-development.

PORTRAITS OF OLDER ADULTHOOD

Key Concerns:[49]

1. Integrity—centers more on the flaws of self; moves toward acceptance that one did the best he/she could in life (integrity)
   ◇ those who can accept self and history tend to be generative; involved in society to be of real help to others
   ◇ identify with their age group and accept self as part of the older generation
   ◇ fight change with less anger; fewer illusions; more wisdom
2. Disengagement vs. activity—well-adjusted adults both disengage and remain active; duality is integrated so that the best of each side is utilized
   ◇ by age 65, adults have detached and do have more passive relations than when at 45–50; still actively involved
   ◇ each person chooses areas for disengagement and activity to fit his/her self-concept
   ◇ death and old age are not perceived negatively
   ◇ affective responses; the give and take of intimacy are now valued as positive traits
   ◇ involves disengagement in one area and activity in another
      —status and achievement for congeniality
      —control for harmony
      —doing for being
      —progress for continuity
      —high aspiration for responsible aspiration level
      —goal pursuits for skill substitution
   ◇ flexibility is essential; ability to adjust depends on external and internal resources
   ◇ new identity forms if one's sense of personal worth is strong
3. Physical changes—task is to transcend the body, finding satisfaction in human relationships and creative mental activity according to one's gifts and state of health
4. Retirement—requires modifications; recasting financial affairs; search for new achievement outlets; leisure time management; adjusting to more present marriage partner; developing a meaning beyond job; reconciliation with death
   ◇ task is to create new roles and find worth in other activities

General Characteristics:[50]

1. Body—lessening in general well-being creates a feeling that one's health is precarious
   ◇ loss of vision in low light
   ◇ loss of hearing in some frequencies
   ◇ fatigue; possible heart problems beginning
   ◇ tendency to body preoccupation
2. Mental abilities—slow but *effective*, depending on state of health
   ◇ load is low compared with power
3. Marriage—continues to be satisfying
   ◇ males assign themselves as boss while females perceive themselves as dominant
   ◇ interdependent, supportive relationship, both hormonally alike can continue active sexual relationship
   ◇ may choose to make change in their life (smaller home, etc.)
   ◇ illness and possible death of partner (average age of widowhood—61)
4. Life review—continues; questions of self-fulfillment continue
   ◇ Have I done all I set out to do/be?
5. Time—continues to be finite; future planning in terms of retirement
   ◇ males: rewrite their past, but have foreshortened future projections
   ◇ physical and occupational changes continue making future unsure
   ◇ possible stress is retirement (poorly planned)
6. Socially—more time spent in leisure pursuits; passive activities according to health
   ◇ more expressive than instrumental activities; hobbies
   ◇ less specific social functions with other people
   ◇ participation is less strenuous; activities for shorter time periods
   ◇ joining community groups without leadership role
7. Personality—more expressive; feelings freely shared; more humanitarian and moral; tactful; reliable
   ◇ males concerned with leaving a legacy; females with helping others
   ◇ both wish to remain independent
8. Male/female difference
   ◇ Males are less mutual; less satisfied; less hostile; mellow; restlessness decreases; happy if past was happy
   ◇ Females are happier, more assertive and self-controlled; express joy even if past was not joyful

Primary Life Tasks of Older Adulthood[51]
(indicative but not exclusive)

Vocation and Career

Adjusting to retirement
Finding new ways to be useful
Understanding Social Security, Medicare, and welfare

Enjoyment of Leisure

Establishing affiliations with the older age group
Finding new hobbies
Learning new recreational skills
Planning a balanced recreational program

Health

Adjusting to decreasing strength and health
Keeping fit
Changing your diet
Having regular medical exams
Getting appropriate exercise
Using drugs and medicines wisely
Learning to deal with stress
Maintaining your reserves

Community Living

Working for improved conditions for the elderly
Giving volunteer services
Maintaining organizational ties

Home and Family Living

Adjusting to reduced income
Establishing new living arrangements
Adjusting to death of spouse
Learning to live alone
Relating to grandchildren
Establishing new intimate relationships
Putting your estate in order

Personal Development

Developing compensatory abilities
Understanding the aging process
Re-examining your values
Keeping future-oriented
Keeping up your morale
Keeping up to date
Keeping in touch with young people
Keeping curious
Keeping up personal appearance
Keeping an open mind
Finding a new self-identity
Developing a new time perspective
Preparing for death

Taken From: Malcolm S. Knowles, *The Modern Practice of Adult Education: From Pedagogy to Andragogy*, rev. ed. (Chicago: Follett Publishing Company, 1980), pp. 263–264.

WORKSHEETS

This section on needs assessments and parish profiles will enable you to look realistically at the composition of your parish and assist you in identifying the types of adult learners you are assisting.

These worksheets may be used for small group brainstorming sessions or for larger group discussion and planning.

What Is Our Parish Already Doing for Adults?

Directions: Assessment needs to be done regarding *actual* parish ministry and programming for the *various categories of adults* belonging to a parish. You may wish to expand this sheet into a series of brainstorming sheets for your pastoral team, planning committee, etc. Be sure to indicate *ministry and programming* that occurs on an individual, small group, large group, and parish-wide basis.

Members in Early Adulthood

Members in Middle Adulthood

Members in Older Adulthood

Married Couples

Engaged Couples

Unmarried Singles

Gay Men and Lesbian Women

Divorced and Separated

Widows and Widowers

Couples with Children

Single Parents

Parents of Infants and Young Children

Parents of Children

Parents of Pre-Teens and Teens

Parents of Children with Special Needs

Physically Handicapped Adults

Mentally Retarded Adults

Grieving Adults

Chronically Ill/Dying Adults

Spouses/Relatives of Chronically Ill/Dying

Military Personnel/Spouses

Unemployed/Unemployable

Retired

Adults Who Work/Career Persons

Racial/Ethnic Groups

Parish Leaders/Lay Ministries Formation

Emotionally Disturbed/Spouses/Relatives

Chemically Dependent/Spouses/Relatives

Unchurched/Alienated/Non-Participating

Adults Caring for Aged in Their Homes

Adults in Family/Personal Crisis

Adults in Transition

Highly Mobile Adults

Immigrants

Non-English Speaking Adults

Poorly Educated Adults

Highly Educated Adults

Grandparents

Infirmed Adults/Adults in Extended Care Facilities

Spouses/Relatives of the Infirmed/Institutionalized

Imprisoned Adults/Spouses/Relatives

Who Are the Adults in Our Parish Community?
(Parish Population Survey)

Directions: Survey your parish population via written survey, house visitation, parish census, evaluation of current census files, etc. Place the total on the space below. (To be used by evaluation/planning committee)

Sex: _____ adult males _____ adult females

Age: _____ 17–22 _____ 23–28 _____ 29–34 (Early Adulthood Population)
_____ 35–44 _____ 45–55 _____ 56–64 (Middle Adulthood Population)
_____ 65–70 _____ 70–80 _____ 80 + (Older Adulthood Population)

Race: _____ White (non-Hispanic origin) _____ Black (non-Hispanic origin)
_____ Hispanic _____ Asian _____ Pacific Islander
_____ Native Alaskan/American Indian

Status: _____ Never Married _____ Married _____ Separated/Divorced
_____ Widowed
_____ Religious/Private Vows _____ Ordained Priests/Deacons
_____ Couples with Children _____ Single Parents
_____ Adoptive/Foster Parents
_____ Parents with Children in the Home—Ages 0–5 Years
_____ Parents with Children in the Home—Ages 6–10 Years
_____ Parents with Children in the Home—Ages 11–13 Years
_____ Parents with Children in the Home—Ages 14—18 Years
_____ Parents with Young Adult/Adult Children in the Home—19 Years +
_____ Adults Caring for Aged/Infirmed in the Home

Highest Level of Education: _____ Elementary School _____ High School
_____ Vocational School _____ Technical School _____ Apprenticeship in Skilled Trades
_____ 2 Year College Degree _____ 4 Year College Degree
_____ Post-Graduate Degree _____ Other _____

Occupational Groupings: _____ Sales _____ Skilled Trades
_____ Professional _____ Clerks/Secretaries _____ Homemakers
_____ Small Business _____ Agriculture _____ Unskilled Laborer
_____ Home-based Business _____ Retired _____ Unemployed
_____ Management _____ Other _____

Participation: Number of Years in Parish _____ 0–5 _____ 6–10
_____ 11–20 _____ founding member
_____ Very Active (weekly) _____ Moderately Active
_____ Occasionally Active _____ Unchurched/Non-Active

For Which Adults Does the Church Express Concern?

Directions: Check off the categories that you think apply.

( ) Men
( ) Women
( ) Young Adults
( ) Aged
( ) Clergy
( ) Religious
( ) Married Deacons and Spouses
( ) Married Couples
( ) Engaged Couples
( ) Unmarried Singles
( ) Gay Men and Lesbian Women
( ) Divorced and Separated
( ) Widows and Widowers
( ) Parents
( ) Parents without Partners
( ) Parents of Handicapped
( ) Adoptive Parents
( ) Foster Parents
( ) Childless Couples
( ) Relatives of Chronically Ill or Dying

( ) Chronically Ill
( ) Infirmed
( ) Grieving
( ) Employed
( ) Career Persons
( ) Unemployed
( ) Unemployable
( ) Retired
( ) Non-English-Speaking Migrants
( ) Immigrants
( ) Racial and Ethnic Groups
( ) Military Personnel
( ) Parish Leaders/Lay Ministries
( ) Physically Handicapped
( ) Emotionally Disturbed
( ) Chemically Dependent Persons
( ) Relatives/Friends of Chemically Dependent Persons
( ) Unchurched and Alienated Persons
( ) Adults Caring for Aged in Their Homes
( ) Other _____

SOME QUESTIONS FOR REFLECTION AND SHARING

1. Why did you check off the items you did?
2. Discuss your reasons for items you may have left blank?
3. What do you think the Church's official response would look like in comparison to your own? Discuss.

For Which Adults Does Our Parish Express Concern?

Directions: Check off the categories that you think apply.

( ) Men
( ) Women
( ) Young Adults
( ) Aged
( ) Clergy
( ) Religious
( ) Married Deacons and Spouses
( ) Married Couples
( ) Engaged Couples
( ) Unmarried Singles
( ) Gay Men and Lesbian Women
( ) Divorced and Separated
( ) Widows and Widowers
( ) Parents
( ) Parents without Partners
( ) Parents of the Handicapped
( ) Adoptive Parents
( ) Foster Parents
( ) Childless Couples
( ) Relatives of Chronically Ill or Dying

( ) Chronically Ill
( ) Infirmed
( ) Grieving
( ) Employed
( ) Career Persons
( ) Unemployed
( ) Unemployable
( ) Retired
( ) Non-English-Speaking Migrants
( ) Immigrants
( ) Racial and Ethnic Groups
( ) Military Personnel
( ) Parish Leaders/Lay Ministries
( ) Physically Handicapped
( ) Emotionally Disturbed
( ) Chemically Dependent Persons
( ) Relatives/Friends of Chemically Dependent Persons
( ) Unchurched and Alienated Persons
( ) Adults Caring for Aged in Their Homes
( ) Other _____

SOME QUESTIONS FOR REFLECTION AND SHARING

1. Why did you check off the items you did?
2. Discuss your reasons for the items you may have left blank.
3. How does you parish assessment compare to your assessment of the Church at large? Discuss.

Which Adults Do Our Parish Organizations Involve?

Directions: Check off the organizations that are currently operating in your parish. Indicate next to each organization the categories of adults that it involves.

NAME OF ORGANIZATION OR ACTIVITY	MEN	WOMEN	BOTH	EARLY ADULTS	MIDDLE ADULTS	OLDER ADULTS
Parish Council						
Education Commission						
Liturgy Commission						
Parish Life Commission						
Spiritual Life Commission						
Finance Commission						
Social Concerns Commission						
Youth Commission						
Youth Ministry						
Peace and Justice; Campaign for Human Development						
Diocesan Pastoral Council						
Deanery Forum						
Food Bank; Hunger Center; Co-op						
Parish Choir; Cantor; Arts; Musician						
Inter-Faith Sharing; Ecumenical Committee						
Community Action Group						
Lector; Eucharistic Ministers						
Ushers; Welcoming Committee						
Meals on Wheels						
Friendly Visitor; Program for Homebound						
Family Ministry; Activities; Retreats						
Neighborhood Fellowship						
Foreign Missions; Evangelization; Society for the Propagation of the Faith						

NAME OF ORGANIZATION OR ACTIVITY	MEN	WOMEN	BOTH	EARLY ADULTS	MIDDLE ADULTS	OLDER ADULTS
Catechetical Ministry catechists, principals, aides, secretaries, A.V., etc.						
RCIA—catechists, sponsors, communications, rituals, participants						
Parish Renewal; Leaders, hosts, and all participants						
Parish Day Care; Early Child Program						
Packaged Programs: Genesis II, Romans 8, Fully Human, Fully Alive, Serendipity Programs, etc.						
Natural Family Planning; Birthcare; Birthright; etc.						
Parish Communications; Newspaper, Bulletin, Flyers, Mailings						
Summer Vacation Bible School						
Engaged Encounter; Pre-Cana; Couples to Couples Ministry						
Marriage Encounter; Marriage Renewal; Couples to Couples Ministry						
Revival; Parish Mission; Parish Week of Retreat						
Days/Evenings of Recollection; Weekly Holy Hour; Parish Retreat Weekends						
At-Home Retreat Program						
Parish Prayer Groups						
Charismatic Renewal Group						
AA/Al-Anon; Chemical Dependency Support Group						
Over-Eaters Group						
Support Group for Chronically Ill; Dying; and Families						
Ministry to the Bereaved						

NAME OF ORGANIZATION OR ACTIVITY	MEN	WOMEN	BOTH	EARLY ADULTS	MIDDLE ADULTS	OLDER ADULTS
Widows and Widowers Group						
Ministry to the Separated and Divorced						
Parents Without Partners						
Hospice for the Dying						
Veteran Organization; Support Group						
Ministry for Unemployed						
Adult Sports Program Fitness Network; Wholistic Health Programs						
Parish Archives; Historians						
Sunshine Club for Ministry to Sick and Infirm						
Adopt-a-Grandparent Program						
Grandparents Club						
Big Brothers/Big Sisters						
Fund Raising Activities; Raffles; Bingo Crew; Pledge Volunteers; Walkathons, etc.						
Parish Census; Mailing; Record Keepers; Collection Crew						
Maintenance; Grounds Committee; Volunteer Cleaning Crews						
Catholic Scouting Programs						
Coaches for Parish Youth Teams; Booster Club						
Church Vocations Committee; Serra Club; Avilas; Theresians, etc.						
Parish Twinning Projects						
Parish Picnics; Dances; Socials; Festivals; etc.						
Weekly Scripture Study at Parish or in the Homes						
Catholic Book Club; Book Discussion Group						

NAME OF ORGANIZATION OR ACTIVITY	MEN	WOMEN	BOTH	EARLY ADULTS	MIDDLE ADULTS	OLDER ADULTS
Film Club						
Speaker-of-the-Month Club						
Community Counseling Opportunities						
Pilgrimage; Regular Novenas; Special Devotions						
Parish Credit Union: Workers and Members						
Parent/Teacher Organizations						
Parent Volunteer Program in Parish School						
Adult Education Planning Committee						
Sacramental Programs: team of presenters, participants (Baptism, Eucharist, Reconciliation, Confirmation, Marriage, Communal Anointing of the Sick)						
Holy Name Society						
Knights of Columbus, Isabella Guild						
Women's Guild, Men's Brotherhood						
Legion of Mary						
Altar and Rosary Society						
Various Adult Education Speaker Series						
Knights and Ladies of St. Peter Claver						
Guadalupano Asociacion						
Right to Life Society						
Parish-Based Ethnic Organization						
Other						

1. In reviewing the adult population of your parish, how do the age groupings compare to one another? (Rank order from 1 to 9 with 1 being the largest population.)

   _____ 17–22 _____ 23–28 _____ 29–34 (Early Adulthood)

   _____ 35–43 _____ 44–55 _____ 56–64 (Middle Adulthood)

   _____ 65–70 _____ 70–80 _____ 80+ (Older Adulthood)

2. In reviewing your current level of programming/organizations, which age groupings are involved the most? the least?

   (Rank order from 1 to 9 with 1 being the largest population.)

   _____ 17–22 _____ 23–28 _____ 29–34 (Early Adulthood)

   _____ 35–43 _____ 44–55 _____ 56–64 (Middle Adulthood)

   _____ 65–70 _____ 70–80 _____ 80+ (Older Adulthood)

3. Reviewing current offerings and organizations, how many are specifically for males? for females? for a mixed grouping?

4. Which areas appear more deficient at this time?
   Which areas need some improvement?
   Which are adequate as they are?
   What are the real needs at this time for a comprehensive parish offering?

5. To which age group(s) do the parish leaders/pastoral team members belong?
   Is there any comparison that can be drawn between the ages of those who make programming/leadership decisions and the types of programs and organizations currently being offered?
   Is each of the age groups represented during the planning and evaluating sessions?
   Is each of the age groups represented in parish leadership positions?
   What can be drawn from this study/reflection/sharing regarding the support and resources provided by the parish for the parish?

Is Human Development Different for Christians?

What makes our growth as persons different from the growth of all other living things is that it takes place by way of consciousness, knowledge, and freedom gained through the presence of God.[52] We experience this presence with a certain intimacy or immediacy inviting the transformation of our attitudes and actions. The Christian vision of human life sees all human development as religious.[53] Faith development and psychosocial development are not seen as opposing elements in Christianity.[54] The challenges of responding to a life with God are not foreign to the challenges of psychosocial development.[55] We are not made up of sacred and secular pieces. Religious development is included in physical, intellectual, emotional, social, and moral development. It is attentive to the dimensions of the holy and the transcendent in all areas of human growth.[56]

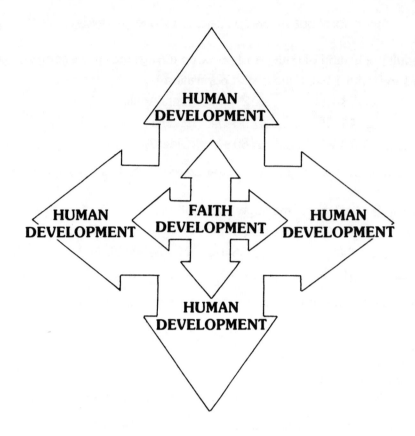

The relationship between psychosocial and religious development is a tension-bearing, paradoxical one. Faith development and psychosocial development make demands on each other. Faith can transform or change our ordinary lives by accepting what is good in them and bringing that to fuller development. It can add the dimension of depth and the holy to what is seen as common. On the other hand, the deepening complexities of each stage of human development necessitate a faith response capable of adequately addressing life's ultimate questions and meanings.[57] This intimate partnership allows for an interpretation of life in which God's activity can be discovered at work within the structures of our psychosocial development.[58] The psychological challenges, crises, and tasks of human development present opportunities and invitations that we, as believers, can choose as graceful and holy.[59] We can choose to respond religiously to the challenges of adult life with attitudes and actions that are psychologically informed and thoroughly Christian.[60]

Developmental crises play a significant role in the interfacing of human and faith development.[61] Crises serve as traffic lights, standing at the crossroads of opposing impulses. We experience crises as painful periods of increased vulnerability.[62] They invite us to re-examine and even reorient our lives. Successfully negotiated crises can lead to growth and further integration of our personalities. How we will respond to a particular crisis is always a free choice. Adults grow through crises rather than being overcome by them. To say that crises are developmental suggests that we are repeatedly challenged to negotiate transitions of loss and gain as a means of growth.

Persons of faith view life's expected and surprising events as religious experiences. The crises and failures that intersect adult life invite the Christian into the paschal mystery. Within the disorientation of crisis the believer can experience the grace of deliverance and the gift of being empowered far beyond personal capabilities and expectations.[63] This sense of being led through crises and repeatedly healed into greater wholeness by God is what makes a crisis religious.[64]

For the Christian, Jesus stands as the sign and guarantor that "negotiated crisis" is the pattern of life in which religious faith is tested and thrives. Jesus is the goal, the psychological ideal of maturity or adulthood.[65] We are invited by baptism to identify our personal experiences of loss and gain with the paschal event of Jesus.

We are challenged to live the Gospel paradox where those who lose their lives live![66] The adult believer actively engages each new crisis with hope, trusting that this process of being emptied of control is a way of growing up into God's possibilities. The surprise, disorientation, fear, anger, and letting go experienced during crises are seen as stepping stones along the road to intimacy, generativity, and integrity.[67]

Faith development challenges us to take an active role in our own psychosocial development. The Gospel message invites us to strike a balance in our personal inclinations, to grow in our ability to love and commit ourselves, to be creative and responsible for what we create, to discover and construct meanings in our lives, and to grow in acceptance and appreciation of ourselves with all our fragility and limitations.[68]

SOME QUESTIONS FOR REFLECTION AND SHARING

1. On a large size sheet of paper draw your lifeline from birth to the present. Divide the lifeline into various age segments: birth to age 5; 6 to 9; 10 to 13; 14 to 18; 18 to 30; 30 to 35; 35 to 40; 40 to 50; and so on.

birth	5	10	13	18	30	35	40	45

2. Draw a running line from birth to the present, indicating the major *peaks* and *valleys* (lows and high points) that you have experienced thus far.

birth	5	10	13	18	30	35	40	45

3. Indicate with words or symbols the *key experiences* of these peaks and valleys. What meaning did these experiences have for you then?
   What meaning do they have for you now?

4. Indicate in words or symbols the times along your lifeline when you sensed that you were having a *religious experience*: a profound feeling of awe, of the presence of God, of the absence of God.

5. How did these significant moments involve a change in your life? Growth? Reassessment? Re-evaluation? Clarification of values? Denial? etc.

6. As you reflect back upon your experiences, can you clearly define or separate times of human growth and development and times of religious growth and development? Explain.

7. How has God entered the heart of your life thus far?
   What have been some of the key events in your life that you would label "calls from God"?
   What are some of your present experiences in which you sense the movement, presence, or call of God?
   How do you feel the tug of the Spirit within you at this time?

It Sounds Like "Inner Growth and Outer Change"[69]

Christian adults participate actively in their own religious development. Embracing personal and communal change is a central challenge of Christian life. There are many ways believers have expressed this dynamic of change—conversion, metanoia, rebirth, transformation, new life, putting on Christ, in the image and likeness of God, the glory of God, etc.[70] In the context of faith development, conversion is seen as a developmental experience occurring over a relatively long period of time in which aspects of our faith response undergo significant change.[71] Blocked feelings are accepted and expressed effectively. Religious knowledge is appropriated into personal meaning. Moral choices begin to reflect personally owned values. Life is appreciated as mystery and gift rather than as an unending series of problems. God is no longer held at arm's length. He is embraced as a relational partner. Once relegated to a two thousand year old event, Jesus becomes a personal, living covenant coming to fulfillment deep within. The Church is no longer blamed or ignored as an institutional "they." It becomes for the believer an active, interpersonal "we."[72] These long-time movements of conversion are nurtured by a lifetime of smaller steps through scheduled and spontaneous choices and events toward psychological maturity and wholeness in the risen Christ.[73]

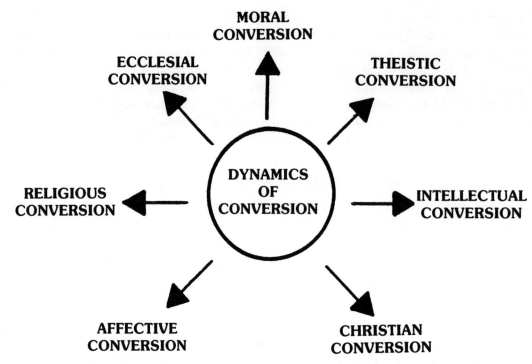

MORAL
CONVERSION

ECCLESIAL
CONVERSION

THEISTIC
CONVERSION

RELIGIOUS
CONVERSION

DYNAMICS
OF
CONVERSION

INTELLECTUAL
CONVERSION

AFFECTIVE
CONVERSION

CHRISTIAN
CONVERSION

A helpful model for understanding the development of faith over the life span is the pattern of a human relationship. In relationships there are exchanges of positive growth and experiences of regression, pain, conflict, confrontation, and reconciliation. There are choices and attitudes that block growth and occasions for deeper insight and appreciation. So it is with our own spiritual life. Light and darkness, joy and sorrow, growth and regression are all part of our journey through the stages of faith.[74]

Stages of faith are styles of knowing and valuing, of composing our relatedness to ourselves, others, and God.[75] They reflect levels of significance and meaning given to these relationships. They involve the appropriation of present, past, and future meaning.[76] Maturity in faith appears to be less a question of fidelity to expectations acquired in earlier years and more a question of faithful adaptation to the different and often confusing challenges that arise during the five or six decades of adult life.[77] "The journey of faith is one in which a life with God colors, influences, and gives deeper meaning to all human activities. The religious person makes the religious dimension of life an explicit one and through this faith transforms all human life and culture."[78]

SOME QUESTIONS FOR REFLECTION AND SHARING

1. Thinking about the present: What gives your life meaning?
   What makes life worth living for you?
   Have you always seen life this way? Explain.

2. At present, what relationships seem most important for your life?
   Are there other persons who at earlier times have been significant in shaping your outlook on life?
   Has the meaning of relationships changed for you?

3. Have you experienced losses, crises and suffering that have changed or colored your life in special ways?
   Have you had significant moments of joy, ecstasy, peak/breakthrough experiences that have shaped or changed your life?

4. What experiences have affirmed your sense of meaning in life? Why? What experiences have shaken or disturbed your sense of meaning?
   Why?

5. Can you describe the beliefs and values or attitudes that are most important in guiding your own life?
   Have your beliefs and values or attitudes always been this way?
   Explain.

6. When you have an important decision to make regarding your life, how do you go about deciding? Have you always made decisions in this way? Give examples. Explain.

7. What feelings do you have when you think about God?
How would you describe God at this time?
Have your religious feelings and understandings about God always been this way? Explain.

8. Who is Jesus for you right now?
How do you feel about this?
Has your understanding of Jesus always been the same? Explain.
Why do you feel this is so?

9. What images does the word "Church" evoke?
What meaning does the Church have for you at this time?
How has your understanding and appreciation for the Church changed over the years?

10. What is your image or idea of mature faith? Explain.

11. Where is your growing edge at the present time?
How do you feel that you are presently changing, growing, struggling?

12. Do you think that there are any similarities between your answers and reflections from above and those of others? Explain. What has been the role of other people in your growth and development? Why do you feel this? Explain. What has been your role? What has been God's role? Explain.

What Would These Stages of Faith Look Like?

James Fowler, an associate professor of theology and human development at Emory University, has developed a stage theory of faith development. Based on ten years of research and interviews with over five hundred persons, his is the first major organization of theological concepts within the framework of the human life cycle.

Fowler sees "faith" as active, a verb. Faith is not something that one does or does not have, but rather a process of becoming. This process is continual growth through stages that are "hierarchical" (increasingly complex and qualitative), "sequential" (they appear one after the other in the life span), and "invariant" (they follow the same order for all persons). It is important to remember that "faithing" is a sacred process involving the action of the Holy Spirit within the context of human life. Moving from stage to stage is not a process of achievement or upward mobility. It is a transformative action of deepening or opening more and more to the light of the Spirit. It is a movement of overlapping waves flowing forward and ebbing backward. Each stage and our unique response to it helps to shape our path toward fullness in the Lord. Each crisis challenges us to stretch beyond our present coping skills, and in so doing to reassess our current self-understanding, basis for personal morality, social integration, capacity for intimacy, view and exercise of authority/leadership, source of motivation, world view, image of God, and image of the Church.[79]

In negotiating these challenges of faith growth, it can be helpful to get a sense of the stages we are living out of by naming the attitudes, behaviors, and understandings we have already outgrown or have deepened. Faith development research can also provide us with a new angle into our current and past experiences. We can become more actively involved in our faith journey being written in the chapters of our life story. We can trust ourselves to the healing rhythm of the ages and stages of life. Renewed consciousness can help us to appreciate the freedom we have in the choices we make each day and remind us of the overwhelming "mystery" that beckons us forth little by little to wholeness.

The research suggests that we are drawn to individuals and groups reflective of our current faith development and can be challenged by exposure to others embodying the next style in the sequence. This seems valid when we consider that our present faith stage is the Spirit-directed, labored-result of collected experiences, insights, reflections, and understandings. We invite one another into wholeness as we share the contents of our living faith story. We spontaneously confront one another as the paths of our journeys intersect throughout the day and in the various settings of our lives. We call each other forth during times of shared doubt, darkness, loss of orientation, and felt meaninglessness. We tug at each other's heartstrings during experiences of shared understanding, profound joy, and resting in mystery. We challenge each other to stretch beyond present investments of trust and commitment, to reassess current self-concepts, and to deepen lived responses of faith. The Spirit shapes and sustains our faith in community.

Windows into the Stages of Faith Development

Stage 0   Undifferentiated Faith   (Fowler)
            Primal Faith   (Ard)
            _____   (Westerhoff)
            _____   (McBride)

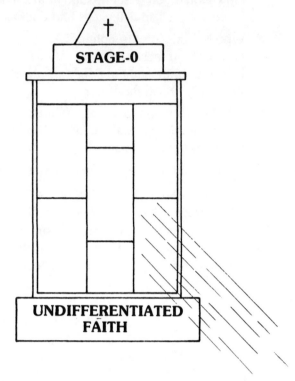

General Characteristics:

◊ pre-faith existence of infancy
◊ negotiation of Trust vs. Mistrust
◊ pre-images

Needed Support:

◊ care of physical needs
◊ warmth and abiding presence
◊ someone loving and trustworthy

Stage 1   Intuitive-Projective Faith   (Fowler)
            Intuitive Faith   (Ard)
            Experienced Faith   (Westerhoff)
            Time of the Poet   (McBride)

General Characteristics:

◊ generally between ages 4–7
◊ children reflect the visible faith of parents
◊ a faith of watching others believe, act, celebrate, and pray to their God
◊ based on feelings of trust toward loved ones
◊ negotiation of Autonomy vs. Shame and Doubt
◊ negotiation of Initiation vs. Guilt
◊ aware of death and sexual differences
◊ no understanding of world view
◊ fundamental loyalty and trust
◊ "Humpty Dumpty not prepared to assert the complexity of life"

Needed Support:

◊ a person of gentleness and trust
◊ being allowed to watch and quietly wonder what is happening
◊ freedom to ask questions as they come up
◊ parents who are aware of the child's God image = parents

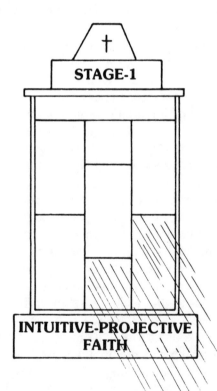

Ministry That Calls This Faith Forth:

◊ baptism
◊ community fellowship
◊ symbols
◊ prayers answered

40

- ◊ nature
- ◊ choir
- ◊ music
- ◊ the arts

Stage 2	Mythic-Literal Faith	(Fowler)
	Narratizing Faith	(Ard)
	Affiliative Faith	(Westerhoff)
	Time of the Reasoner	(McBride)

General Characteristics:

- ◊ generally between ages 7–12
- ◊ the faith of childhood
- ◊ ability to distinguish past, present, future
- ◊ imagination curbed by logic
- ◊ authority exists for service to others
- ◊ broader world view; broader loyalties
- ◊ negotiation of Industry vs. Inferiority
- ◊ takes on beliefs of persons other than parents
- ◊ rise of narratives and stories of faith
- ◊ stories of faith most meaningful
- ◊ transformed primal images of Numinous and Ultimate Environment
- ◊ primary dynamic of belonging and learning the story
- ◊ "Humpty Dumpty had a great fall"
- ◊ reason aids life's complexity

Needed Support:

- ◊ community-involvement, tasks, belonging
- ◊ good family model—belonging model
- ◊ clear limits
- ◊ clear behavioral norms
- ◊ knowing how to act
- ◊ rites of time and passage
- ◊ acceptance even when unacceptable
- ◊ peer activities involving new learning

Ministry That Calls Forth This Faith:

- ◊ sense of community and fellowship
- ◊ use of symbols
- ◊ storytelling
- ◊ prayer experiences
- ◊ singing, music, shared prayer
- ◊ witness from significant others
- ◊ group involvement in activities, projects, service
- ◊ support family model of belonging
- ◊ clear limits, norms for behavior
- ◊ "rites of passage" celebrations
- ◊ acceptance even if nowhere else
- ◊ youth retreats, suppers, games
- ◊ good physical atmosphere that speaks of belonging
- ◊ baptism

◊ nature study
◊ catechetical activities
◊ use of the arts

Note: Some adults stay at Stage 2.

Stage 3	Synthetic-Conventional Faith	(Fowler)
	Synthetic Faith	(Ard)
	Searching Faith	(Westerhoff)
	Time of the Ecumenist	(McBride)

General Characteristics:

◊ begins in adolescence for most persons
◊ ability to see self as others do
◊ reflection on the meanings of life stories (theirs and others)
◊ negotiation of Identity vs. Role Confusion
◊ building a new world view from different and contradictory experiences from within and without
◊ ever-increasing perception of life's complexity
◊ authority comforting when it explains
◊ religious community of faith functions as a support system
◊ a dynamic of questioning and experimentation begins
◊ conforming to the "gang"
◊ faith begins to synthesize life's increasing complexity
◊ new stories, a new people, new community of faith; find stories of themselves/others meaningful
◊ reflects on the meanings of things
◊ needs skills to doubt, to disagree, to question, to challenge faith they and others have had
◊ beginning of real discernment

Needed Support:

◊ a community of other searchers
◊ a questioning pastoral minister
◊ classes, small groups
◊ being challenged to have an answer
◊ support of their desire to know
◊ correlation of faith and reason supports
◊ environment that supports searching
◊ structured external environment where it is easy to do the expected
◊ people who accept the fact that all questions can't be answered

Ministry That Calls Forth This Faith:

◊ small groups to be with, building a community
◊ gathering searchers together

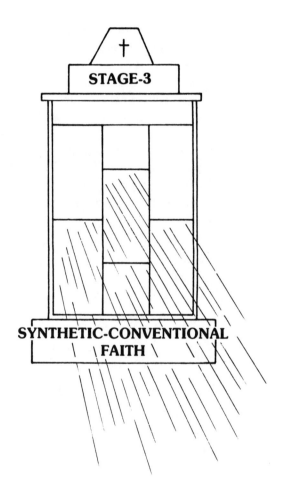

STAGE-3

SYNTHETIC-CONVENTIONAL FAITH

- ◇ asking good questions
- ◇ support their desire to know
- ◇ correlate faith and reason
- ◇ structured, easy-to-do environment
- ◇ opportunity to be with mature people who understand that many questions take a lifetime to answer

Note: Adults who are strongly influenced by peers are in Stage 3.

Stage 4	Intuitive-Reflective Faith	(Fowler)
	Individuative Faith	(Ard)
	Searching Faith	(Westerhoff)
	Time of the Personalizer	(McBride)

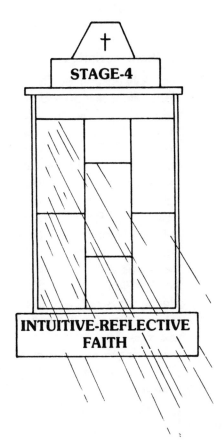

General Characteristics:

- ◇ tends to arise in early adulthood
- ◇ negotiation of Intimacy vs. Isolation
- ◇ focus on adult responsibility for one's own commitments and beliefs
- ◇ doubting, questioning, and rejecting traditional assumptions
- ◇ development of individual values
- ◇ new identity in relation to new center of values; does not depend on how others see them
- ◇ images of power, master story
- ◇ reflective construction of ideology; formation of a personal dream
- ◇ translating symbols and images into concepts that can be put into words
- ◇ breaking open symbols for their kernels of meaning
- ◇ inner drive toward personal synthesis
- ◇ tendency to neglect tensions or absolutize one of the poles
- ◇ faith with its dynamics if questioning and experimentation goes on

Needed Support:

- ◇ situations of having to make a decision
- ◇ called to witness; to go public
- ◇ feedback for personal questions
- ◇ support in coming to terms with limitation and mortality
- ◇ other committed people
- ◇ process for recalling experiences
- ◇ help in discovering the commitments that are being made

Ministry That Calls Forth This Faith:

- ◇ small groups to be with—in community
- ◇ opportunities to share with other searchers

- ◊ pastoral ministers who ask good questions
- ◊ being challenged to find answers
- ◊ supporting their desire to know
- ◊ "easy-to-do-the-expected" environments in which to share
- ◊ sharing with mature people who understand that many questions take a lifetime to answer

Note: Some adults may choose to remain in Stage 4.

Stage 5	Conjunctive Faith	(Fowler)
	Paradoxical-Consolidative Faith	(Ard)
	Owned Faith	(Westerhoff)
	Time of the Tension Bearer	(McBride)

General Characteristics:

- ◊ generally arises in adults of mid-life and beyond (seldom before age 30 and often never reached)
- ◊ negotiation of Generativity vs. Stagnation
- ◊ finds life and deep meaning in apparent contradictions
- ◊ strong appreciation for truth expressed in paradox
- ◊ realizes that justice transcends clan, nation, and religion
- ◊ new respect for symbols, rituals, traditions, and beliefs of religion, noting limits
- ◊ committed faith of adult life
- ◊ deals well with the issues of intimacy and authority in adult life
- ◊ identity does not depend on how others see them
- ◊ incorporates the integrity of positions other than one's own
- ◊ responds beyond race, class, ideological boundaries
- ◊ intergenerational responsibility for the world begins; new vocational horizon, new theology
- ◊ primary dynamics of personal commitment and action

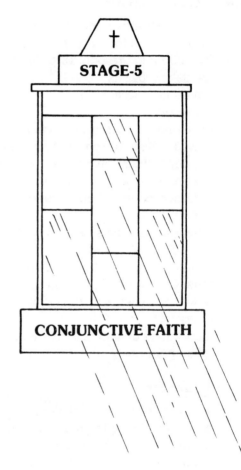

Needed Support:

- ◊ role models; community of like-minded people
- ◊ opportunities for experienced faith; reflection
- ◊ celebration of community
- ◊ experiences of success, "I can change the real world"
- ◊ liturgy, sacraments, critical study
- ◊ opportunities for exercising responsibility

Ministry That Calls Forth This Faith:

- ◊ strong role models giving lived witness in the community

44

◊ shared reflection, prayer, spiritual reading
◊ times for recalling heroes of the past, present, and future
◊ celebrations of the faith community; peak experiences of faith
◊ liturgy, sacraments, commitment ceremonies
◊ critical study and questioning sessions
◊ ministry within the faith community
◊ help in seeing how their ideas, hopes, values, past, present, etc., fit together and are explained in the Gospel message of Jesus
◊ reflections into the commitment they are living

Stage 6	Universalizing Faith	(Fowler)
	Universalizing Faith	(Ard)
	Owned Faith	(Westerhoff)
	Time of the Universalizer	(McBride)

General Characteristics:

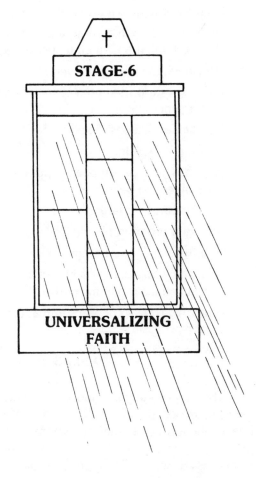

◊ persons reaching this stage are fairly rare; spiritual giants; often martyrs; saints, prophets . . .
◊ usually would not arise until the late adult era
◊ committed faith of the adult life
◊ one deals well with the tensions of intimacy and authority in adult life
◊ symbols and images into concepts and words
◊ respects symbols, tradition, ritual, beliefs
◊ faith is universal; identification beyond self with God as a felt reality
◊ new partnership with God in and for the world
◊ commitment and action
◊ unifying world vision; kinship with all beings
◊ puts "Humpty Dumpty back together again"
◊ a simple, lucid, interpreter of life
◊ his/her presence is often seen as a grace/inspiration to others
◊ accepts differences, flexible, just
◊ negotiation of Integrity vs. Despair

Ministry That Calls Forth This Faith:
◊ strong role models of adult faith
◊ meeting together in community
◊ reflection, prayer, spiritual reading
◊ celebrations of that faith community
◊ positive feedback
◊ liturgy, sacraments, commitment ceremonies
◊ opportunities to lead the community to deeper faith experience, justice
◊ celebrate how their hopes, values, past, and present are all part of the Gospel message of Jesus, creating the kingdom now and for the future

N.B.

A more complete understanding of the stages of faith development can be gained by reading the following works from which the preceding summary statements were gleaned.

James W. Fowler, *Stages of Faith Development: The Psychology of Human Development and the Quest for Meaning* (San Francisco: Harper and Row, Publishers, 1981), pp. 119–213, 269–291.

R.T. Gribbon, "Faith Development Theory: A Tool For Ministry," *Action Information Newsletter*, Vol. VII, No. 3, ed. Celia Allison Hahn (Washington, D.C.: Alban Institute, Inc., 1981), pp. 6–8.

Alfred A. McBride, O. Praem., *Creative Teaching in Christian Education* (Boston: Allyn and Bacon, Inc., 1978), pp. 85–112.

Gwen Kennedy Neville and John H. Westerhoff, III, *Learning Through Liturgy* (New York: The Seabury Press, 1978), pp. 160–170.

SOME QUESTIONS FOR REFLECTION AND SHARING

1. What does "personal journey of faith" mean to you at this point in your life?
   What does "communal journey of faith" mean? Explain. Compare.

2. How can personal and communal dimensions of faith be linked? in your own life? in your parish?

3. Take some time and write down your personal faith history. Go back as far as you can remember.

4. Do you recognize any "chapters" in your journey of faith?
   Do these chapters address any of Fowler's stages of faith? Explain.

5. Do you think faith communities go through stages of faith development together?
   Do you think the Church universal experiences this movement? Explain.

6. How have the changing events of your life affected your faith in God? (Refer back to your faith history.)

7. What has supported your growth in faith?
   ◇experiences? Explain.

   ◇particular persons? Explain.

   ◇mother? Explain.

8. How has your parish been supporting adults as they grow in faith?
   What needs to be done?
   ◇in the parish-at-large?

   ◇in adult program planning?

   ◇during actual adult programs or activities?

9. Does the whole area of faith development need to be taken into account more seriously in your planning of adult education in the parish? Explain.

10. What might be some steps in that direction? Brainstorm.

What Is the Religious Journey of Early Adulthood?

The task of early adulthood is to find a place in adult life. This means, among other things, taking on a sex role, an occupation, and a world view. The challenge of this period comes with the problems of this period. It takes the form of intimacy ("Whom am I with?") and mutuality ("How am I with others?"). Both challenges involve a willingness to risk one's newly found identity, to risk being changed, and to risk coming to a different awareness of self.[80] The impulses against these two challenges are isolation and independence. Synthesis of these tensions enables a capacity for self-disclosure, self-awareness, active listening, mutuality, understanding the motives behind needs and feelings, expression of personal need and respect for the needs of others, and translation of ambitions into actions.[81] These capacities make commitment possible.[82] As early adults allow their beliefs and ideologies to flow from their renewed sense of identity, deeper expressions of faith become evident (Fowler's Individuative–Reflective Stage). Embodying intimacy and mutuality necessitates a constant emptying of self (kenosis). Kenosis is the faith task of early adulthood.[83]

Fidelity to personal and professional commitments surfaces new tensions.[84] Early adults (generally after age 30) now find themselves being pulled between conflicting loyalties.[85] The paradox of life and the paradox of the Gospel imperative stand front and center. As early adults accept paradox as an essential characteristic of all truth and move beyond their own needs, another stage of faith begins to unfold (Fowler's Conjunctive Stage). Persons living out of this stage remain committed to a religious view of life even though they realize that it neither answers all questions nor meets all the dimensions of their personal dream.[86] An awareness of personal doubt and confusion along with life's woundedness challenges the young adult to readjust and expand his/her personal dream/ideals/goals. This emptying process is so demanding that many new adults choose to live around it, assuming a stance of alienation, dissatisfaction, and disidentification. They become religious drop-outs, failing to align their faith with their search for personal identity and satisfying intimacy.[87] Early adults who are able to live out of a conjunctive faith stage begin the task of reworking their personal past with an attitude of reconciliation. This "healing of memories" allows early adults to forgive themselves and others.[88] In so doing, they choose a faith response of discipleship, learning from the Master, Jesus.[89]

SOME QUESTIONS FOR REFLECTION AND SHARING

1. What words best summarize your feelings and experiences of early adulthood?
   What issues were key for you and your peers during this stage of adult life?
   (Note: If you are presently a young adult, answer these questions from your current perspective.)
2. What did you find supportive or most helpful in negotiating the challenges of early adulthood?
   What resources did you wish you would have had during that period of your life?
3. Did you and your peers respond in the same way to the tasks of intimacy and mutuality? Similarities? Differences? Successes? Failures? Explain.
4. What do intimacy and mutuality mean to you now?
   Has your understanding and appreciation changed?
   Are you still dealing with these issues?
5. What are the operating myths surrounding the issues of intimacy and mutuality?
   How do these issues fit into the Gospel living and human wholeness?
6. Name the early adults you interact with each day.
   Do you hear these issues and struggles in their concerns and actions?
   Is there any way that you can support or resource these people in their journey toward wholeness in the Lord?

What Is the Religious Journey of Middle Adulthood?

The main issue of middle adulthood is the choice between generativity and self-centered concern.[90] Adults in the middle period of life are faced with the question, "Why am I doing this?"[91] This question causes them to re-evaluate their personal dreams and vision, the quality of care they are giving for what they have created, their present attitudes toward power and productivity, and the degree to which they are responsive and responsible.[92]

Middle adults react in many ways to the question "Why?" Some react with acceleration, trying to prove themselves and denying their age. Others regress into earlier stages of behavior. Still others escape into their work, sex, or alcohol. The mature response to the question is an acceptance of limits. The real crisis of middle adulthood is authenticity.[93]

Authenticity demands that middle adults approach themselves and others with reconciling compassion. It demands a resolution of inner polarities (young-old, destruction-creation, masculine-feminine, attachment-separation, energies directed toward self and a few intimates-nurturance for future generations).[94] Middle adults are called by the Spirit to deeper interiority. They are challenged to heal the gap between their world and God and between their body and spirit.[95] They must break out of the protective myth of their dreams and grow more deliberately into the paradox of the Gospel.[96] Fowler states that the religious development of midlife generally centers around stages 4, 5, and 6, depending upon the size of the adult's generative vision and lived compassion.[97] All three stages of faith represent some degree of reconciliation and kenosis.

The ministry of the middle adult years is that of diakonia (belief and gifts in action for others according to the Christian dream or vision).[98] Middle adults live their faith out of an integration of faith roots given by family and Church, the beliefs of others, personal answers to ultimate questions, and the acceptance of personal limitations and giftedness.[99] The challenge of middle adulthood is to arrive at a mature expression of faith that is wholly personal.[100] It is understandable that midlife adults are the most active in worship, education, and service programs.[101]

SOME QUESTIONS FOR REFLECTION AND SHARING

1. What words would you use to describe the concerns, feelings, and challenges of middle adulthood?
   (Note: If you are a young adult, respond to these questions from the perspective of what you have observed about middle adults you know.)
   In your own life experience, how many of the words you listed would hold true?
   Do you think other middle adults would respond similarly? Explain.

2. Did you experience a transition or undergo a crisis upon entering middle adulthood?
   Have your peers negotiated entrance into middle adulthood in the same ways you have? Similarities? Differences?

3. What are the losses, gains, paradoxes, and religious invitations of middle adulthood? Why might researchers say that the middle years are a time of reconciliation?
   Do any of your experiences speak to this issue?
   Do you think there is any validity to a statement like "crisis of limits" or "paradox" when referring to middle adulthood? Explain.

4. Has you relationship with God changed now that you are a middle adult? If you have experienced changes, why? What changes?
   Has there been a change in your attitude toward other aspects of life—moral decision-making, church, community, relationships, marriage/singlehood, values, sexuality, etc.?
   If so, how would you explain these changes?

5. What does middle adulthood have to offer the human community, the faith community? early adults? older adults?

6. What are the major issues that concern you now as a middle adult?
   What types of support and resources do you feel are needed at this time?
   Do you feel that these resources and supports are available to you?

7. Name the middle adults you know and interact with.
   What resources do you have to assist and support them in their faith journey?
   What insights and resources might they offer you?

What Is the Religious Journey of Older Adulthood?

The period of older adulthood is the zenith of life, for it is a time in which integrity becomes manifest.[102] Older adults wrestle with questions of integrity: "Of what value am I?" "What does human life mean?" "How am I to deal with suffering? Change? Loss?" "Why must I die?"[103] Older adults are challenged to turn inward to find a meaning and wholeness that will make it possible to accept death.[104] As in earlier periods of life, the choice of letting go enabled transition to the next stage of psychosocial development and belief. So, too, in older adulthood. Letting go enables the final stage of Christian adulthood—resurrection. As older adults ready themselves for the crisis of death and the radical healing of resurrection, they are invited to see their deep questions illuminated by the images of tradition and in the faith of those with whom they live.[105]

The developmental tasks of older adulthood are: establishing a sense of self-worth less dependent upon productivity or role, reaching a deeper acceptance of one's own life, and coming to terms with the diminishments and losses of aging.[106] If these developmental tasks are met, the older adult can look over the past events of life with feelings of satisfaction and actualization resulting in integrity. Unable to negotiate these tasks, many older adults fear death and bear a sense of personal failure for a wasted life.[107] They live in despair.

Unfortunately, our culture is full of biases against aging. We have trained ourselves, and we train younger people to fear older adulthood. We train older people to apologize for age. We retire people at 60, 62, or 65, and tell them that for the next twenty years they can't work anymore and are useless. The message is affirmed by our commercial advertising, inaccessible buildings, non-extended family units, micro-chip pace, competitive mentality, recall of health and living benefits, and rapid explosion of senior care facilities where elders are stored until they die. Elders themselves fulfill the prophecy assuming old age is diminution rather than culmination, living death rather than spiritual transcendence, and retirement from contribution rather than offering new possibilities for nurturance and permanent fulfillment. Our society and its systems cripple older adults far worse than the infirmities of aging.

In order to embrace integrity, older adults need sufficient autonomy to function, agreeable relationships with other people willing to help where needed, a reasonable amount of bodily and emotional comfort in the physical environments, adequate stimulation of their minds and imaginations, mobility to permit variety in their surroundings, and some form of intense involvement with life to avoid preoccupation with death.[108] Older adults are challenged with the task of re-membering themselves in order to grow into wholeness. They need the same resources that their earlier selves needed in growing. In assessing the meaning of all that has happened, older adults develop the gift of wisdom.

Fowler describes the last stage of faith development as Universalizing Faith. This faith stance is exercised by those whose lives are so attuned to the ultimate meanings of life that their faith expression is beyond self-interest, taking on a universal quality.[109] Fowler suggests that few adults live out of the stage of Universal Faith. Could this be the result of a lack of skills, resources, and support provided early, middle, and older adults?[110] Do the operating myths of adulthood in our capitalistic society maim the vision of maturing adults?[111] Do our current operating models of Church encourage adult believers to remain in developmental holding patterns?[112] These and many more questions need to be explored regarding the religious journey into adulthood.

Older adults need to tell their particular and generational story of life with God (anamnesis).[113] In being able to tell their story, older adults gain self-acceptance. They hear the meaning of their story in its telling.[114] In reflecting with loved ones over the cost of their story now nearly told, older adults can recognize that their lives have significance transcending death.[115] They can approach their remaining years with forgiveness, appreciation, and hope.

SOME QUESTIONS FOR REFLECTION AND SHARING

1. What qualities do you associate with aging?
   What qualities would you like to possess as an elder in the community?
   Why?
   Do you know or have you known individuals who embody these gifts as older adults?
2. What fears and misgivings do you have when thinking of growing old, facing retirement, and embracing death?
   Are there connections between these fears and your current faith life?
   Are there connections between these fears and the culture in which we live?
   Where do your current thoughts and feelings about growing old come from?
3. What will you like most about aging?
   What aspects do you look forward to?
   Do you recognize these hopes embodied in elders you know?
4. What are the hopes and fears of the elders you presently know?
   What are their felt needs at this time?
   How do you see yourself presently responding to those needs?
   If you do not see yourself responding, why not?
5. What do you think is the Christian meaning of growing old?
   Do you own that meaning?
   What should it mean to grow old among Christians?
6. Can you think of some ways that we can begin to change the cultural meanings of aging and improve upon the supports needed for growing old with faith and dignity?

CHAPTER III

Life Cycles and Learning: New Trends in Passage

Connections Between Changes in the Adult Life Cycle and Learning

Most adults over thirty can remember a time when the sequence of education was quite simple. We began our formal education as youngsters, graduated from high school as teens, sought final job preparation in college, technical school, or apprenticeships, and moved into lifetime occupations as adults. It was easy sailing from then on into promotions and eventual retirement with our pension plans and Social Security. The question "What are you going to be when you grow up?" would generally require a single answer. Once we found our niche in the world, we were set for life. Passages, accepted as functions of age, were so automatic that we needed little support in handling them.[1]

Within the past few decades, technology has created an explosion of change resulting in more specialized occupations. Lifetime jobs are now a rarity. A recent news broadcast suggested that the distance between one generation and another in 1985 was five years. Not too long ago the changes an adult could expect to negotiate were stretched out over a forty to fifty year period. Now that same change load is compacted into five. Increased longevity has increased the time-span of social change to seventy years and beyond. Today's adult must negotiate the same amount of change in his/her lifespan that would have taken earlier generations fourteen lifespans. It is no longer reasonable to define education as a process of transmitting what is known to children and adolescents. Education, of necessity, must be lifelong.[2]

It is not surprising that the rate of participation in formal and informal adult learning has exceeded the rate of population growth in this country.[3] Yet, of the 126 million possible adult learners, not all choose to participate in adult education.[4] For this reason, adult educators have been exploring the causes of adult learning. Insights into the causes of adult learning can aid pastors and their planning committees in developing comprehensive programs with appealing learning activities that will enliven and empower their adult communities.[5] Insights into the motivation behind adult learning can help pastoral leaders support adults in their lifelong learning.

Categories of Adult Learners

Researchers have discovered different categories of adult learners. While most learners approach education with mixed reasons or motivation, a central emphasis is usually discernible.

CATEGORIES OF ADULT LEARNERS[6-7]	
Goal-oriented Learners	Learners who learn to accomplish specific goals
Non-directed Learners	Learners having no specific goals; learning for its own sake
Social Learners	Learners seeking to improve their contacts and relationships with others
Stimulation-seeking Learners	Learners looking for relief from boredom and routine
Career-oriented Learners	Learners who learn because of occupational interests
Life Change Learners	Learners who see learning as a means of coping with change in their lives

SOME FACTORS LEADING ADULTS TO LIFELONG LEARNING[8-9]	
Strong relationships with parents	Stimulation by others to continue learning
Positive experiences with past teachers and schooling	Adequate finances/resources to permit lifelong learning
Familiarity with libraries as important resources	Desire to change career or occupation
Good information networks	Highly motivated
High past success	Ability to recognize needs/interests

REASONS WHY SOME ADULTS CHOOSE NOT TO INITIATE LIFELONG LEARNING[10]	
Situational Barriers	Lack of time, lack of transportation, lack of child care, geographic location
Dispositional Barriers	Feeling too old, lack of confidence, fear of failure, boredom with past schooling
Institutional Barriers	Poor scheduling, cost vs. value, poor location, offensive facility

COMPARISON OF REASONS FOR LEARNING[11]	
17%	83%
–Learn for the sake of the learning experience	–Learn for the sake of something else
–Regard the learning activity itself as the benefit desired	–Are learning to obtain some other benefit
–Receive satisfaction during the learning experience, apart from the later effect	–Receive satisfaction from a later effect
–Regard the process of learning or the possession of knowledge to be its own reward	–Want some reward for learning
–Learning is its own justification	–Learning is utilitarian
–Learning is the end	–Learning is a means

Changes in the Adult Life Cycle Influence Learning

Researchers have found that more adults learn to make career transitions (56%) than for all other reasons combined. Family (16%) and leisure transitions (13%) compete for a distant second place. Art (5%), health (5%), religion (4%), and citizenship transitions (1%) hardly make an impact.[12]

More than 90% of all adults state that changes in career (56%) and family life (36%) trigger their need for learning. It appears that career and family clocks set the time for learning in adult life. Changes in health (4%), religion (2%), and citizenship (1%) are not frequently mentioned as having a significant impact on the times that ongoing learning is chosen. Research suggests that the timing of learning is largely determined by specific life events that permit or force adults to learn. "To know an adult's life schedule is to know an adult's learning schedule."[13]

Other Factors Affecting Learning Choices During Life Change

Research suggests that there are demographic characteristics which affecting adults as they experience life changes and consider learning as a means of coping and/or obtaining skills.[14]

Demographic Characteristic	Effect on Learning Choices[15]
Sex	–Men learn more often than women because of career changes –Women learn more often than men because of family, leisure, or health transitions
Age	–Adults under age 65 learn chiefly because of career transitions –Adults over age 65 learn chiefly because of leisure and family transitions
Status	–Adults who are single, married, or divorced learn because of career transitions –Widowed adults learn mainly because of leisure and family activities
Education	–Adults who have attended 4-year colleges learn most often for their careers –Adults who have attended 2-year colleges or high school learn more often for other reasons—leisure, family
Income	–As income rises, adults learn more often for career reasons
Occupation	–Workers and students learn primarily to make career transitions –Homemakers and retired adults learn primarily to make leisure and family transitions –As occupational level rises, adults learn more often for career reasons

Clocks Setting the Timing for Learning in the Adult Life Cycle[16]

1. Changes in Careers

–being hired
–starting a new job
–having an existing job changed/adapted
–advancement offer/higher income
–promotion/need new training
–retiring

2. Changes in Family

–providing food
–providing different shelter
–providing different clothing
–managing shifts in income/expenses
–caring for other family members as changes occur

3. Changes in Leisure

–increase in leisure time
–change leisure activities requiring new skills
–decrease in leisure ability
–moving away from leisure activity center
–loss of leisure income

4. Changes in Artistic Life

–increased leisure time
–long-delayed interests
–coping with change

5. Changes in Personal Health

–recovery from illness/injury
–maintaining fitness
–improving health styles
–adjusting to loss of health/deterioration

6. Changes in Religion

–deepening relationship with God
–need to learn more about God's plan for their life
–religious experience
–need to learn new values
–new ways to spend increased time
–study the meaning of their religion as adults
–changes in family/health

7. Changes in Citizenship

–immigration studies
–community volunteerism

CAREER AND FAMILY CLOCKS SET THE TIMING FOR ADULT LEARNING

53

WHERE DO ADULTS LIKE TO LEARN?[17]	
28%	Learn completely on their own
17%	Learn guided by their employer
14%	Choose institutionally-directed learning at colleges and universities
12%	Choose local settings—religious institutions, community colleges, local adult education centers
While Engaging Transitions	More likely to choose a college, place of employment, professional organization for support and learning
When Not Engaging Transitions	More likely to be found at religious institutions, in private lessons, or completely on their own
While Engaging Career Transitions	Prefer formal learning settings
While Engaging Family Transitions	Prefer religious institutions, assistance from family and friends, or private instruction
While Engaging Religious Transitions	Prefer religious institutions, assistance from family and friends, or private instruction
While Engaging Health Transitions	Are as likely to learn on their own as to participate in programs offered by community agencies
While Engaging Art/Leisure Transitions	Are generally supported through private lessons and independent learning

WHAT TIME DO ADULT LEARNERS PREFER TO LEARN?[18]	
40%–60%	Prefer evening hours
Non-workers	Prefer morning hours
Most adults	Dislike weekends with the exception of religious learning if connected with the worship service

WHAT TOPICS DO ADULTS PREFER TO LEARN?[19]	
Self-directed learners	Any topic is an object of learning
75%	Prefer to learn things that have practical applications; "how-to's"—business, home repairs, travel, skills, etc.
17%	Desire to learn intra-self topics such as: religion, philosophy, art, music, and psychology

WHAT RESOURCES DO ADULTS PREFER IN LEARNING?[20]	
Most adults (73%)	Prefer to plan their own learning
27%	Prefer to utilize groups, professionals, friends, and non-human resources such as books to direct their learning
Self-planned learners who are better educated	Prefer to use books as important resources for gathering their information
Self-planned learners who are less educated	Prefer to use electronic media sources and direct contact with persons as important sources for gathering information

"The value of knowing what kinds of transitions cause adult learning lies in being able to predict *what* they are likely to learn. The value of knowing what kinds of *events* trigger adult learning lies in being able to predict *when* they are likely to learn."[21] Knowing what adults need and when they will need it is invaluable for parish ministry and program planning.

Summary of the Relationship Between Change in the Adult Life Cycle and Learning

◊ Adults learn on their own and with the support of others and institutions.

◊ Adult participants do differ from those choosing not to learn.

◊ Most adults do not choose learning for its sheer enjoyment.

◊ Adults learn in order to cope with change in their lives.

◊ Learning can precede, accompany, or follow transitions.

◊ All aspects of adult life surface as needs for learning.

◊ The number of transitions in each life area correspond exactly to the amount of time devoted to that area.

◊ One can track down educational needs by knowing how adults spend their time.

◊ Adults who learn to cope with change more often learn several things at once, more often learn career skills, and more often choose formal learning situations.

◊ Every adult who chooses to learn because of a transition can point to a significant event that signaled, precipitated, or triggered the transition and the learning.

◊ Triggering events occur unevenly in several areas of adult life—namely, career and family.

◇ The number of triggering events in each life area correspond closely to the amount of time adults spend in each life area.

◇ While the topic an adult chooses to learn is always related to the life transition requiring that learning, the topic is not always related to the event that triggered the learning.

SOME QUESTIONS FOR REFLECTION AND SHARING

1. How would you define learning?
   Do you think other adults would define it this way also?
   Did you understand learning in this way as a child? as a teenager?
   Explain.

2. Think of a recent learning experience that you really enjoyed!
   What was it that you really liked about it?
   Describe.

–topic	–place	–cost	–other
–instructor	–activities	–time	
–people involved	–materials used	–results	

3. Think of a recent learning experience that you really disliked!
   What was it that you really disliked about it?
   Describe.

–topic	–place	–cost	–other
–instructor	–activities	–time	
–people involved	–materials used	–results	

4. How many new things have you chosen to learn thus far this year?
   Why do you choose to participate in learning?
   What are some other reasons adults might choose to learn?

5. What are some of the things you have chosen to pass up this year in terms of learning?
   What are some of the reasons you have had for choosing not to participate in a learning opportunity?
   What are some of the reasons other adults might have in choosing not to participate in a learning opportunity?

6. In what ways do you learn best? Do you enjoy learning?
   Do you think other adults have learning preferences also?

7. Is all your new learning facilitated by an instructor/guide?
   Are there ways that you have devised for learning on your own?
   Are there ways that other adults you know have devised for learning?

8. What do you think is the best way for adults to learn?
   Do you think other adults would agree with you?

9. How is your parish already addressing the following transitions of adult life:

–career/work transitions?	–artistic transitions?
–family transitions?	–religious transitions?
–leisure transitions?	–citizenship/community membership
–personal health transitions?	transitions?

10. Put the above transitions in rank order as you think they should be addressed by the Church; by your parish; by the message of the Gospel; by the challenge of Christian life.

11. Brainstorm: What might be some of the ways that your parish community could address these transition needs in addition to what already is being done?

12. How do you think the demographic make-up of your parish has affected attendance at past parish programs/activities?

    –age   –education   –status   –other
    –sex   –occupation   –economic level

13. How might the parish take its demographic make-up more seriously in future planning?

Adults *Are* Their Experiences

Although we all see qualities of adulthood in ourselves and in those around us, adulthood can never be completely defined. Each of us is a unique story being told by the Father in the name of Jesus. We are all parts of Mystery unfolding in time. Researchers in biology, education, human development, philosophy, psychology, and sociology have been studying adult persons for quite some time. Together they have singled out some common characteristics that affect adult learners. A sensitive, balanced awareness of these characteristics can help parish planners in the design and effectiveness of adult learning activities. Lack of sensitivity and awareness defeats the goals of any parish effort and insults those who choose to participate.[22]

In considering these characteristics, it is important to remember that no one characteristic is more important. Each is interdependent, giving context and contrast to all the others. To engage or ignore one is to affect all the rest. Concern for the adult as a learner necessitates concern for all the aspects of the adult person.[23]

A Reflection on Adult Learning Characteristics

Directions: Listed below you will find fourteen characteristics common to adult learners. Next to each characteristic, questions are offered for reflection and planning. You may approach the questions individually as a facilitator of adult learning. You may choose to approach the questions as part of a parish adult education planning/evaluation committee.

ADULT LEARNING CHARACTERISTIC	QUESTIONS FOR REFLECTION AND PLANNING
1. Adults can learn.[24–26]	–Are all adults in the parish regarded as possible learners?
	–Are the intellectual gifts of each learner capitalized on during the learning experiences?
	–Are early adults challenged to acquire new knowledge?
	–Are middle adults challenged to apply their learning to themselves and others?
	–Are older adults encouraged to share their integrated wisdom on the topic?
	–Are the learners free to learn at their own pace?
	–Does planning allow for the various speeds at which the learners approach the topic at hand? Is there room for quality instead of quantity?

ADULT LEARNING CHARACTERISTIC	QUESTIONS FOR REFLECTION AND PLANNING
	—Is the learning environment conducive to the needs of the older learner: ◇ adequate illumination? ◇ elimination of glare? ◇ effective use of visuals? ◇ slow and clear speech? ◇ adequate volume? ◇ writing surfaces? ◇ support/review hand-outs? ◇ comfortable furniture?
2. Adults are their experiences.[27–33]	—Are learners invited to share their related experiences? —Are learners invited to reflect upon the meaning of their experiences in light of current experience? —Are the learners' experiences used as teaching tools? —Are learners' experiences used as resources for the entire learning community? —Does the facilitator build a bridge between the learners' experiences and the topic(s) at hand? —Are mistakes used as learning resources?
3. Adults use their experiences in evaluating daily occurrences and in making decisions for the future.[34–38]	—Are the learners invited to share their past understandings, opinions, biases, concerns, and questions regarding the topic at hand? —Are the learners invited to evaluate how the learning process is going for them? —Are the learners encouraged to give feedback, reactions, etc., to what is being presented? —Are the learners invited to participate in values clarification, stem completions, and forced choice experiences, allowing their biases, opinions, etc., to surface? —Does the facilitator assist the learners in interpreting their learning experiences? —Does the facilitator use an active and varied methodology during the learning experience, allowing the learners to experience and modify the learning task according to their gifts and interests? resourcing each other? gaining competence? growing in self-esteem? feeling success? feeling valued?

ADULT LEARNING CHARACTERISTIC	QUESTIONS FOR REFLECTION AND PLANNING
4. **Adults develop in a lifelong search for personal identity.**[39–45]	—Are learners invited and encouraged to evaluate the meaning of experiences? —Are adults challenged to express the dualities hidden within a consideration? personal tension points? —Is there an attempt to make a connection between the learners' needs and the content-at-hand? —Are they encouraged to tie class experiences into the meaning of their lives? —Can learners discover their self-understandings by sharing their understandings as resources for each other? —Do the learners feel that they are being talked down to? —Is the stance of the leader one of facilitation or "keeper of the content/wisdom"? —Are the learners encouraged to be self-directing? —Is the learning climate respectful, allowing learners the space to express how they really feel about themselves? —Are the learners asked what they want or need in the learning experience? —Are the learners involved in the planning, execution, and evaluation of their learning? —Does the leader regard himself/herself as a learning reference? as a co-learner? —Does the leader remember that each adult begins at a different starting point in the learning process? Are these individual differences accepted? respected? —Is the learning experience seen as the place to try out new skills? wrestle with dualities? make needed adjustments in views and behavior?
5. **Needs, interests, and values create an affective and cognitive base for an adult's learning goals.**[46–53]	—Are a learner's goals seen as a summation of the meaning an adult gives to his/her life? needs? interests? or values? —Are adults encouraged to adjust and modify their goals as they move through the learning experience? —Are the learners given the freedom to change as part of the learning experience?

ADULT LEARNING CHARACTERISTIC	QUESTIONS FOR REFLECTION AND PLANNING
	—Are adults encouraged to appreciate change as part of adult life?
	—Are the learners' personal needs, interests, values, and goals actively engaged in the learning experience?
	—Are learning experiences problem-centered rather than theoretically oriented?
	—Do the participants feel that the learning outcomes will have meaning for them in their lives? How do you know?
	—Is the learning experience directly related to the felt needs of the learner? Has planning been around those needs?
	—Are the learners' current knowledge and strengths recognized and taken into account before needs, gaps, deficiencies, and new directions are examined?
	—Are needs uncovered and goals set through mutual sharing, interaction, and negotiation?
	—Are the learning goals or directions stated by the learners in terms of what they want to know? feel? be able to do?
	—Are new goals and directions allowed to emerge throughout the learning experience, rather than being established only at the beginning?
	—Are the learners involved in problem-solving activities, case histories, reflective questionnaires, and critical incident activities allowing for flexibility in the learning process?
6. Adult learners expect comfort. [54–57]	—Are your learners physically comfortable? How do you know? Do you ask them?
	—Are learners' habit needs met: food? beverages? ash trays? proper ventilation for non-smokers? ability to walk around? control of noise level?
	—Do you attend to learners' body language? Do you take comfort readings throughout the session?

	—Are learners encouraged to interrupt and express their needs: to break? to clarify? to discuss? to change methods? to resolve conflict? to change the environment? to provide a comfort item that is missing? to slow or increase pace?
	—Are learners' habit needs part of your planning and evaluation? Is this cost added to the budget along with other needed supplies?
	—Is your learning space warm and welcoming? comfortable? encouraging an adult atmosphere?
	—Are the learners able to take control of their learning environment? move furniture? adjust lighting? raise or lower the temperature? etc.?
7. **Relational preferences influence an adult's self-concept and affect his/her choices and actions during a learning situation.** [58–62]	—Are you aware of introverted and extraverted relational preferences among your learners?
	—Are you aware of the adults who learn best through perceiving? judging? intuiting? or sensing?
	—Do you give choices in relational settings to accommodate various relational styles among the learners?
	—Are you aware of which adults enjoy leading and which do not?
	—Are you aware of which adults prefer to share and which prefer to listen?
	—Are you aware of which learners prefer/learn best while working in groups and which prefer/learn best by working alone?
	—Do you plan according to your learners' relational needs or according to your own as leader?
	—Are you aware of dominant learners vs. submissive learners in your learning community?
	—Do you create a variety of relational environments to meet the various needs of your learning community?

ADULT LEARNING CHARACTERISTIC	QUESTIONS FOR REFLECTION AND PLANNING
	–Do you use a variety of methods to meet the learning styles of your learning community?
	–Do you really consider the social climate in your planning? Do you foster a climate where problems can be identified, discussed, resolved?
	–Are learners encouraged to respect each other's relational preferences?
8. **Adult learning is affected by the contexts in which the participants live.** [63–64]	–Do you know the contexts in which your learners live?
	–Do you maximize the benefits of the context in learning experiences?
	–Do you use gender, ethnicity, group affiliation, socio-economic factors, community history, etc., as doors to learning? as barriers?
	–Are the assumptions of the learner explored and recognized before introducing new views? different ways? etc.?
	–Do you recognize the learners as they really are?
	–Are you aware of your own social context? How does this compare with that of the learners? Are you a barrier? How can you share your context without creating hurdles no one can negotiate?
9. **Adults have strengths and weaknesses that may or may not be modified as a result of learning experiences.** [65–66]	–Do you invite adults to act out of their strengths or force them through activities to act out of their weaknesses?
	–Do you respect an adult's desire to act out of strengths? Do you gently help adults try out new strengths, areas they once considered weaknesses?
	–Do you give your learners the freedom to choose when they will risk their weaknesses?
	–Do you plan activities so that experiences of discomfort will be followed by experiences of comfort, success, affirmation?
	–Are your learning activities built step-by-step, moving from the known to the unknown? from security to risk?

ADULT LEARNING CHARACTERISTIC	QUESTIONS FOR REFLECTION AND PLANNING
10. Adults have different learning and communicating styles.[67–72]	—Are you aware of which learners think and prefer learning inductively? deductively?
	—Are you aware of which learners prefer listing information? black-and-white presentations? step-by-step directions?
	—Are you aware of which learners enjoy an unstructured receiving of information? prefer to discuss ideas? need time to mull things over before drawing conclusions?
	—Are you aware of which learners are risk takers? love to experiment? listen until they understand the gist of an idea and then take off on their own?
	—Are you aware of which learners decode written and oral communications into symbols/mental pictures? enjoy well-presented presentations? like substance?
	—Are you aware of your own learning style and preferences? Do you teach and plan only in the ways you like to learn? Do you provide for the diversity of learning styles in your group?
	—Are the methods you use consistent with the goals of the program? the abilities of the learners?
	—Are the learners able to articulate, clarify, formulate questions, formulate answers? for themselves? for others?
	—Are the learners given the opportunity to work with ideas? to work with the learning process? to work with each other?
	—Are opportunities planned wherein learners can try out new ideas? new processes? new behaviors? Can they express their feelings about them as well?
	—Are learners given space to make mistakes?
	—Are learners given time and the means with which to reflect upon what they have learned? what ideas and experiences have meant to them personally?

ADULT LEARNING CHARACTERISTIC	QUESTIONS FOR REFLECTION AND PLANNING
11. Adults may not always attend the learning experiences to which they have committed themselves or in which they have expressed interest.[73-77]	—Are you aware of the many social systems to which your adult learners belong: family, social, work, civic, professional, etc.?
	—Do you recognize that all learners will not be able to attend all sessions and plan them accordingly? Does each session build on the one before and also act as an independent unit?
	—Do you give a brief review of the previous session before beginning new material for those who were absent? Do you recognize that this review will also be of help to those who were in attendance? affirming their presence/progress? allowing time for questions or clarification?
	—Do you prepare summary sheets/summary outlines for those who can only be with you from time to time?
	—Are you conscious of the number of roles you ask learners to assume during the learning experience? too many so as to frustrate? too few so as to insult?
	—Do you invite adults to use their various roles as resources for one another?
	—Are learners free to step out of their daily roles if they so choose? If learners are expected to try out new roles, are they given time to try them? Do you repeat the role in several sessions/activities?
	—Do you force learners into roles in which they are uncomfortable?
	—Are you sensitive to the time demands of your learners? Do you stay within the negotiated time frame? If the time frame changes, do you ask the advice of the learners? Are options given for those who find the time frame impossible? (independent study, guided study, etc.)
	—Do you assist learners in changing gears? Are older learners asked to help younger learners? (learn how to mentor by doing it)
	—Do you know the gifts and needs of your learners? Can you capitalize on their gifts while helping them meet their own needs?

ADULT LEARNING CHARACTERISTIC	QUESTIONS FOR REFLECTION AND PLANNING
12. Adult learning is enhanced when the learning climate fosters self-esteem and interdependence.[78-80]	—Do learners feel respected, accepted, and valued by you and their fellow learners? —Is everyone encouraged to exercise openness of self rather than concealment of self? —Are differences in the group acknowledged as resources? —Are learners allowed to make mistakes and not to know? Are leaders allowed that same right? —Does the atmosphere promote collaboration and support rather than competition and judgment? —Is everyone's experience, attitudes, and knowledge recognized and built upon? —Is confrontation permitted? Do learners and leaders have the right to disagree? to question? to challenge? —Are learners greeted and addressed during the learning experience in ways that model interdependence? —Do you try to embody and create a spirit of mutuality, respect, and light-heartedness?
13. Adults look for practical consequences.[81-85]	—Can learners apply what they learn to their real lives? —Is the curriculum built around their real needs? life problems? interests? —Is the learning experience task-, problem-, or growth-centered? —Are the learning experiences used to promote the individual learner's self-discovery? discovery of personal meaning? —Are learners encourged to trust themselves as well as their external resources? —Are learners assisted in integrating external knowledge with their own personal meanings? —Do you encourage the belief that the sum total of everyone's insights, questions, ideas, and knowledge is far greater than one individual's discoveries? —Do you tolerate ambiguity during the learning process? Are you pleased when new questions follow a learning experience?

ADULT LEARNING CHARACTERISTIC	QUESTIONS FOR REFLECTION AND PLANNING
	—Do you provide ways in which the learners can demonstrate the practical and immediate application of their learning? for themselves? for others? —Do you begin new sessions with the applications, meanings, and insights that learners have discovered between sessions?
14. Adult learning is enhanced when learners evaluate their own learning outcomes, learning skills, and needs for more learning.[86–89]	—Do you help the learners move from self-defined concepts to self-defined goals? —Do you support and encourage self-initiated learning? —Do you guide learners in defining their own goals? in maintaining discipline as they move toward them? in assessing progress once reaching it? —Is evaluation approached as a cooperative process? —Is the emphasis of evaluation on self-evaluation? —Do you conclude learning experiences by inviting the learner to reflect on what he/she wants or needs to do next? —Do you foster discussions helping the learner examine his/her processes? —Do you provide tools with which the learners can evaluate their own levels of participation? competency?

For further insight into adult learning theory read: Judy-Arin Krupp. *The Adult Learner: A Unique Entity.* Manchester, CT: Adult Development and Learning, 1982. These fourteen characteristics and the accompanying questions have been largely adapted from this work.

CHAPTER IV

Educating Christian Adults

The Relationship Between Adult Religious Education and Development in the Adult Life Cycle

Adults are concerned with the here and now. They are also concerned with the meaning of their experiences. Religious education assists Christian adults in negotiating their present challenges by gently plumbing the questions and conclusions of their past memories and future hopes. It sifts the content and contexts of their journeys, separating pebbles of meaning from the sands of time. It probes present assumptions, motives, values, and needs, offering models for reflection and sources of support.

Adult religious education recognizes that the complex factors of human development are the touchstones of the Spirit. For this reason, it can never speak of religious development without attending to its human matrix. The Scriptures reflect this partnership well. The Hebrew and Christian Scriptures abound with images of human/religious passage, transition, and growth:

death . . . life/resurrection
brokenness . . . wholeness
woundedness . . . healing
birth . . . rebirth
bondage . . . freedom/deliverance
lack of growth . . . on-going change/transformation
discord . . . peace
promise . . . fulfillment
darkness/doubt . . . light/understanding
division . . . unity
unbelief . . . belief
hardness of heart . . . renewed hearts
despair . . . hope
aimlessness . . . journey
entering baptism . . . living out of one's baptism
alienation . . . belonging/community
emptiness . . . fullness
fear . . . courage
confusion . . . wisdom
chaos . . . order
lost . . . found
rejection . . . cornerstone

These images in the lives of our fathers and mothers of faith, in the life of Jesus, and in our own lives give meaning to the on-going process of development in the adult life cycle.

Religious education helps adults in imaging God's possibilities in their choices.[1] It challenges adults to grow closer to their experiences, to name their feelings and convictions, and to discover the Sacred unfolding deep within them. It points to the nudge of the Spirit in experiences common to all believers: fear of death, desire to live and grow, search for meaning, longing for happiness and fulfillment, need for security, struggle for freedom, yearning to love and be loved, etc. It reverently explores the unique themes and variations of each individual adult's being, creating, loving, forgiving, growing, sharing, doing, caring, thinking, listening, celebrating, receiving, following, etc. Both the content and the process of adult religious education reflect the belief that spiritual growth occurs when adults see that all their experiences on a human level are reflections of a reality that exists in God and in their relationship with God.

SOME QUESTIONS FOR REFLECTION AND SHARING

1. When is it that you find yourself most aware of God, faith, the religious dimension? Explain.

2. When do you find yourself seeking God, deepening your faith response, looking for support or answers from religion? Explain.

3. Spend some time drawing your personal faith journey. You can expand on some of the ideas you might have developed in earlier sections of this workbook. Take a look at the biblical passage statements below. Would any of them be apt descriptions for stages of your journey? You might want to write them in as you go along.

> death . . . life/resurrection?
> brokenness . . . wholeness?
> woundedness . . . healing?
> birth . . . rebirth?
> bondage . . . freedom/deliverance?
> lack of growth . . . on-going change/transformation?
> discord . . . peace?
> promise . . . fulfillment?
> darkness/doubt . . . light/understanding?
> division . . . unity?
> unbelief/disbelief . . . belief/commitment?
> hardness of heart . . . renewed heart?
> despair . . . hope?
> aimlessness . . . journey?
> being baptized . . . living out of one's baptism?
> alienation . . . belonging/community?
> emptiness . . . fullness?
> fear . . . courage?
> chaos . . . order?
> being lost . . . being found?.
> rejection . . . cornerstone?
> others you can think of . . . ?

If you are working through this exercise with others you might want to share aspects of your faith journey. Share only those parts that you are comfortable in sharing. Be respectful of the sharing of others. There may be some persons who will not be able to share at this time. No one should feel forced.

4. Which biblical passage statements do you think adults in early adulthood would experience? in middle adulthood? in older adulthood? Why?

5. Do you think that the insights gained during this reflection would have anything to say to adult religious education planning? program development? content? Explain.

6. Do you think that the insights gained during this reflection would have anything to say to worship/paraliturgical celebrations in the parish? Explain.

7. What do you think is the relationship between adult religious education and development in the adult life cycle in your parish at this time?
What would you like it to be?
What steps might be taken to realize this vision?

Education Toward Christian Adulthood

One of the most significant ministries of the local parish is education toward Christian adulthood. Education toward adulthood implies moving from dependent to interdependent styles of ministry and learning. Is your parish moving in this direction? Are you, as an adult educator or planning committee member? Where do you stand along the following continua? Where would your parish and its current adult ministry fall? You are invited to use this tool as a means of personal and communal evaluation. It might be interesting to mark each continuum with two different colors—one for the parish's ministry and one for your own.

1. Conception of Adulthood

—"an assumed condition"
—a chronological/biological/legal fact
—a noun
—qualities of adulthood—rational thinking, factual, economically productive, independent, competitive, successful, individualistic, self-actualized, master of life and world
—death is seen as the cruel destroyer that attacks at the end of life
—there are distinct roles—children play, youth study, adults work
—childhood and youth are to be moved away from; separated by categories

—"a lifelong process"
—a psychological ideal
—an adjective descriptive of qualities
—qualities of adulthood—integration and synthesis of opposites: rational/non-rational, self-direction/spontaneous reaction, control/receptivity, life/death, success/personal weakness, giving/receiving, interdependence and mutuality, struggling and striving/letting go, growing deeper, individuality/community, wholeness and justice, befriending the world and life
—death is seen as helper in making us receptive, gentle, caring; death is present in all of life's activities; death is an experience of entire community
—all ages are called to play, study, and work throughout life; role biases fall away
—the qualities and presence of children are the key test to adulthood; integration of everyone in a life-giving, transforming community of mutuality

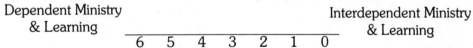

Dependent Ministry
& Learning
Interdependent Ministry
& Learning

6   5   4   3   2   1   0

2. Conception of Education

–"transmission concept"
–a process of transmission of knowledge and culture
–indoctrination of beliefs about the faith and Bible approved by established authority
–"orthodoxy"
–the Church teaches; protective, defensive, circumscribing attitudes about beliefs
–strongly legalistic, paternalistic style of authority
–normative doctrinal tradition

–"personal growth concept"
–a process of guiding the learner to fullest potential as a whole person
–learner is provided with guidance and resources in discovering the facts and beliefs about the Bible and faith which have meaning
–"orthopraxis"
–persons are encouraged to stand on their own two feet spiritually and accept responsibility for their own beliefs and ethical decisions
–heuristic—open to questions and doubts about the validity of present beliefs and moralizing
–self-directed and self-regulating

Dependent Ministry & Learning _____6__5__4__3__2__1__0_____ Interdependent Ministry & Learning

3. Aim of Education

–"formative"
–to gain learner acceptance of facts, skills, attitudes, and beliefs which the culture deems important for the learner to have
–to teach what to learn and think; how to know
–the learners are formed or molded according to a particular paradigm

–"formative and reformative"
–to help the learners develop their fullest potential/capacities and to use them not only to exist in the culture but also to change it
–to continue the nurturing process throughout life
–to teach how to learn and think; how to question and find out
–learners become actively involved with a particular paradigm, examining and evaluating it against others and against their personal experiences

Dependent Ministry & Learning _____6__5__4__3__2__1__0_____ Interdependent Ministry & Learning

4. Educational Focus

–"acquisition of subject matter"
–the product of learning
–teaching subject matter
–to know the right answers

–"what takes place inside the learner"
–the process of learning
–teaching learners
–to know how to ask important questions and to go about finding the answers

Dependent Ministry & Learning _____6__5__4__3__2__1__0_____ Interdependent Ministry & Learning

70

5. Conception of Learning

–"an external process"
–learning is determined by outside forces: the skill of the teacher, quality of reading materials, discipline, etc.
–the teacher govens what is learned

–"an internal process"
–learning as an internal process involving the total person (intellectual, emotional, psychological interplay)
–the learner governs what is learned

Dependent Ministry & Learning
$\qquad \underline{\quad 6 \quad 5 \quad 4 \quad 3 \quad 2 \quad 1 \quad 0 \quad}$
Interdependent Ministry & Learning

6. Educational Objectives

–formulated by the teacher
–formulated in terms of development of ability to recall information and to conform to prescribed behavior (target points)

–mutual negotiation by the learner and the teacher in formulating learning objectives to meet the learner's needs
–formulated in terms of development of competencies (direction of growth)

Dependent Ministry & Learning
$\qquad \underline{\quad 6 \quad 5 \quad 4 \quad 3 \quad 2 \quad 1 \quad 0 \quad}$
Interdependent Ministry & Learning

7. Methodology

–"discursive"
–non-participative in-put followed by questions; one-directional
–dependence on directions of others in learning
–"telling" theological-scriptural-liturgical things
–activities leading to mastering the norms and beliefs of the religious tradition
–the teacher stands outside, above the assembly of the learners

–"relational dynamics within community"
–active learner participation (listening teams, reaction panels, buzz groups, mutual input, mutual questioning)
–mutuality, self-direction based on needs and styles of learning community
–activities to stimulate a process of critical reflection, examining the norms and beliefs of the religious tradition: moving out, over, back, and down into lived experiences
–the teacher joins the learning community

Dependent Ministry & Learning
$\qquad \underline{\quad 6 \quad 5 \quad 4 \quad 3 \quad 2 \quad 1 \quad 0 \quad}$
Interdependent Ministry & Learning

71

8. Role of the Teacher

–to transmit a body of content/new knowledge	–being a resource/guide to self-discovery; encourager; consultant
–role of authority: judge, controller	–to facilitate the interaction between the learners and their environments
–diagnosis of learner needs	
–plan learning activities and programs	–engaging with the learners in constructing situations in which individuals experience the satisfaction of their needs and goals for effective behavior
–sharing answers and questions that the teacher feels ought to be raised	
–using the teacher's experiences in giving examples	
–basis for planning programs may be the teacher's need to discuss certain content areas	–to involve the learners in assessing their needs and goals, formulating their educational objectives, choosing and executing suitable methods, and evaluating learning outcomes
–to transmit the knowledge reflective of the needs of the institution	
	–to facilitate the learners in sharing their experiences as examples and resources
	–to invite a process of dialogue and reflection; listening to the questions and answer the learners raise
	–to provide experiences that will demonstrate the need for knowledge before presenting it in activities

Dependent Ministry & Learning

Interdependent Ministry & Learning

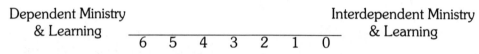

6 5 4 3 2 1 0

9. Role of the Learner

–to receive, accept, absorb content	–self-directing inquiry, creativity
–dependent, conforming, initiative	–to be open to lifelong change and lifelong learning
–to be open to evaluation	
–an experience of youth; formal schooling	–active participation, mutual resourcing in the learning process
	–mutual evaluation, rediagnosis of needs
	–learning in a variety of settings all through life— formal experiences, self-directed experiences, at work, on retreat, from all others

Dependent Ministry & Learning

Interdependent Ministry & Learning

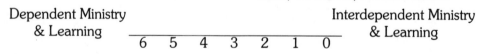

6 5 4 3 2 1 0

10. Learning Outcomes

–"dependent believers"	–"maturing believers"
–the ability to know and recall the information transmitted	–the ability to think, understand, integrate, create, perform, reflect
–conformity of the learner's behavior to the attitudes and beliefs transmitted	–an intellectual understanding that religion is the result of guided, owned, self-discovery in community
–an intellectual understanding that religion is derived from others	
–a religious community that is dependent, more conforming, more imitative	–a religious community that is more self-directing, more inquiring, more creative, prophetic
	–critical thinkers who react to teachings

—spirit of obedience and acceptance of authority
—little integration between the subject explored/
 taught and the lived behavior of the learner
—the teacher's expectations/outcomes

—a change in behavior effected by the experience
 of the learner; those who influence change have
 the prestige in the eyes of others
—the learner's expectations are the outcomes

Dependent Ministry   Interdependent Ministry
    & Learning   6   5   4   3   2   1   0   & Learning

11. Climate

—"authoritative"
—climate established and maintained by the teacher
—highly structured; competitive
—rigid school model; formality; semi-anonymity;
 status differentiation between teacher and
 learners, among learners
—dull, routine, institutional environment

—"democratic/communal"
—climate established by the teacher and co-
 learners; educative community
—mutual resourcing; collaboration, involvement,
 interaction
—feeling of acceptance, respect, support,
 friendliness, informality, known by name, valued
 as an individual, everyone seen as gifted for
 others
—sensitivity in modeling other adult environments
 where sharing takes place; aesthetic quality
 considered

Dependent Ministry   Interdependent Ministry
    & Learning   6   5   4   3   2   1   0   & Learning

12. Evaluation

—standardized testing; content testing
—measured in terms of mastery of approved
 content
—competitive rewarding; grading

—evaluation based on units of change in behavior;
 evaluation of the objectives of the learning before,
 during, and after the learning experience
—value tests, diaries, solutions to case problems,
 situational projective tests, observation,
 internship, feed-back, etc.

Dependent Ministry   Interdependent Ministry
    & Learning   6   5   4   3   2   1   0   & Learning

13. Content

—"sacred vs. profane"
—restricted in scope to theological, scriptural,
 liturgical issues
—approved content
—content determined by the teacher/institution
 according to the perceived needs of the learners
—content is presented according to the logic of the
 subject matter
—focus is on content units/blocks

—"religion as a quality of all experiences"
—all topics are seen as having religious implications;
 all experiences are touched by the sacred;
 wholistic approach
—content is determined by the life tasks, interests,
 and educational needs of the learner in dialogue
 with the teacher and the faith community
—content presentation involves sequencing
 according to learner readiness

—content is generally not integrated by the learners into their lived behavior

—"orthodox position on development of doctrine"

—a stance on development of doctrine as mere translation of the original deposit and its applications, thus discouraging the emergence of maturing belief

—acceptance of approved doctrines, values, attitudes, and bodies of information is encouraged by manner of presentation/transmission

—doctrines solve all questions pertinent to all studied issues

—interprets Church development against the background of detailed directives which "faithful" Christians follow obediently; narrow and confining

—content presented with little freedom and little adaptability to new demands

—focus on problem units

—content is woven into lived experiences, enlightens conscience, is evident in lived behavior/conversion

—"organic position on development of doctrine"

—a hermeneutic stance inviting reunderstanding, rethinking, re-experiencing the meaning of the Word, the teaching

—a stance which embraces faith-consciousness and the lived experience of Christian people; favors the emergence of maturing believers

—content is determined with the learners in terms of a "maturing Christian person" and on the basis of "Christian living"

—doctrinal statements are presented as conditioned by time and flexible enough to give way to new expressions

—creative interaction with experienced problems and doctrine is encouraged

—greater appreciation of the possibilities offered by unforeseen challenges; challenges offer the Spirit the opportunity to lead

—fidelity to doctrine allows room to think; "thinking through" is presented as necessary for the maturing Christian (teacher and learner)

	Dependent Ministry & Learning							Interdependent Ministry & Learning
		6	5	4	3	2	1	0

14. Model of Church

—"institutional"

—reactive, constrictive, circumscribing patterns of authority

—paternalistic; protecting the faithful from harm

—normative doctrinal tradition

—adults draw from the faith of the Church

—ministry "to"

—magisterium urgently authenticates developments in contrast to corruption

—permits believers to understand the doctrines which are taught with their logical implications and applications, and to express them in their own words

—designated leadership; hierarchy

—a structured organization with rules

—"multidimensional":

Renewed Institutional

—restoration of New Testament patterns of authority

—restatement of tradition

—continuity in Catholic teaching

People of God/Body of Christ

—interior gifts and graces of the Spirit are found in all members

—a community of faith sharing gifts and vision

Sacrament

—Church as a sign of God's presence and activity

—union of formal and informal worship and education

–the Church has the power to teach, sanctify, and judge; clericalism
–theologians are loyal but critical defenders of Church teachings

–finding God's activity in human experience, in nature, in social reality

Herald
–Church as assembly listening and responding to the word of God
–calling of individual lives, societal structures to prayerful study, conversion, and witness

Servant
–active and dynamic presence in the world; world mission
–grappling with social issues and structures; shared praxis

Discipleship
–continuity of life and belief with Jews and early Christian community
–all Christians are lifelong disciples including the official ministers of the Church
–stress on unity and mutual support
–synthesis between Christian and worldly values
–learning community
–spiritual relationship with Jesus

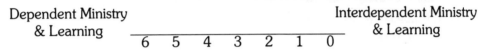

Dependent Ministry & Learning   6 5 4 3 2 1 0   Interdependent Ministry & Learning

N.B.

For a detailed explanation of each of the poles described in the preceding continua, read:

Elias, John L. "Ecclesial Models of Adult Religious Education." *Christian Adulthood: A Catechetical Resource 82*. Ed. Neil Parent. Washington, D.C.: United States Catholic Conference, 1982, 3–9.

Elias, John L. *The Foundations and Practices of Adult Religious Education*. Malabar, FL: Robert E. Krieger Publishing Company, 1982.

Knowles, Malcolm S. "An Adult Educator's Reflections on Faith Development in the Adult Life Cycle." *Faith Development in the Adult Life Cycle*. Ed. Kenneth Stokes. New York: W.H. Sadlier, Inc., 1982, 63–83.

Knowles, Malcolm S. "A Theory of Christian Adult Education Methodology." *Christian Adulthood: A Catechetical Resource 82*. Ed. Neil Parent. Washington, D.C.: United States Catholic Conference, 1982, 9–16.

Knowles, Malcolm S. *Self-Directed Learning: A Guide for Learners and Teachers*. Chicago: Follett Publishing Company, 1975.

Knowles, Malcolm S. *The Modern Practice of Adult Education: From Pedagogy to Andragogy* (rev. ed.). Chicago: Follett Publishing Company, 1980.

McKenzie, Leon. *Adult Religious Education: The 20th Century Challenge*. West Mystic, CT: Twenty-Third Publications, 1975.

McKenzie, Leon. "Foundations: The Scope, Purposes and Goals of Adult Religious Education." *Christian Adulthood: A Catechetical Resource 82*. Ed. Neil Parent. Washington, D.C.: United States Catholic Conference, 1982, 17–22.

McKenzie, Leon. *The Religious Education of Adults*. Birmingham: Religious Education Press, 1982.

Moran, Gabriel. *Education Toward Adulthood: Religion and Lifelong Learning*. New York: Paulist Press, 1979.

Schaefer, James R. "Tensions Between Adult Growth and Church Authority." *Christian Adulthood: A Catechetical Resource 82*. Ed. Neil Parent. Washington, D.C.: United States Catholic Conference, 1982, 22–32.

1. Looking at your overall personal ministry stance, where are you in terms of moving from dependent to interdependent styles of ministry and learning?
   Name some factors that have contributed to your current position.

2. Comparing these responses to your ministry of five years ago:
   What transitions, if any, are recognizable?
   Have these changes been for the better?
   What factors have contributed to this change? Explain.
   What factors have detracted from this change? Explain.

3. It might be helpful to share your results with other pastoral or planning team members.
   How do your personal responses differ? How are they similar? Explain.

4. Where would you like your personal styles of ministry and learning to be in five years? Why?
   What will you need to realize this vision/dream?

5. As a pastoral team/planning committee: Where would you like to be in your shared styles of ministry and learning in five years? Why?
   What will you need to realize this vision/dream together?

6. Looking at your overall parish assessment: Where is your parish faith community in terms of dependent and interdependent styles of ministry and learning?
   Name some factors that have contributed to this current position.

7. Can you remember five years ago? What was your parish's style of ministry and learning then?
   What transition, if any, is recognizable?
   Name some factors that have contributed to that current position.

8. As you, your parishioners, pastoral staff, and planning committee dream for the future: Where would you like the parish to be in its communal style of ministry and learning? Explain.

9. What specific steps can you take right now to begin that future?
   —personally?
   —as a leadership team?
   —as a member of the faith community?

The Relationship Between Adult Religious Education and Secular Learning

Adult religious education does not try to compete with secular offerings in the area. Nor does it limit itself to the sacred, affirming the duality that tries to separate the sacred from the secular, the body from the spirit, the holy from the ordinary. The challenge of adult religious education is to begin where the learners experience themselves to be and to shed the light of faith on their problems, challenges, and developmental tasks/interests. The function of religious bodies is to determine what areas of adult development need special treatment from a religious point of view.[2] Solid religious education does not attempt to pour God into the experiences of adult life, but rather to assist the Christian adult in recognizing the holy that has always been active there. Adults need to discover that God never stops dreaming of their unlimited growth possibilities and that his creative hand is active in the accomplishments and crises of life. Adult religious education is challenged to link the needs, interests, values, and goals of adult learners with the biblical, theological, and spiritual heritage of the Church. Catechists help adults explore the countless images, symbols, and models of human potential found in the Scriptures. Adult religious education is challenged with the task of strengthening adults as they journey in faith through human and Christian development.[3]

Catechesis can help adults live out their decisions, prepare them for the crises of life, and assist them through these crises. (NCD #184)

The Scope and Content of Adult Religious Education

Since all of life is sacred, all learning is religious.[4] "The content of adult catechesis is as comprehensive and diverse as the Church's mission. It should include those universally relevant elements which are basic to the formation of an intelligent and active Catholic Christian and also catechesis pertaining to the particular needs which adults identify themselves as having." (NCD #185) Through baptism all Christians are called to give service in the name of the Lord. All Christians are ministers. All the baptized are challenged to strengthen the body, to build the kingdom, and to live in response to the word. Growth into Christian adulthood is crucial to this ministry. Adult catechesis, therefore, explores all areas that nurture and affect this growth.[5]

How the Parish Identifies Content Areas for Adult Religious Education

The surfacing of content areas for parish adult religious education is a multi-dimensional challenge. There are many starting points. Many people need to be involved. The process for determination of content is an unending one. The many aspects of the plan that each parish will devise will be unique to that faith community. There are no easy, one-size-fits-all answers or programs, nothing you can buy and merely plug-in once a week. Unfortunately many parishes have already tried that easy fix, misusing Genesis II, Romans VIII, Parish Renewal, the RCIA, Serendipity Programs, and, most recently, video tapes. Each of the above mentioned are good vehicles for adult religious education, but they were not intended to be nor could ever become a parish's total adult education ministry.

Earlier in this chapter you explored your parish population and current adult programming/organizations. Building on this base, you are invited to begin brainstorming concerning areas of content. In order to begin the process, you are invited to do a little dreaming. If you are exploring this area with others, follow-up sharing sessions would be of great value.

NCD Paragraph Quotes Taken From: *Sharing the Light of Faith: National Catechetical Directory* for Catholics in the United States (Washington, D.C.: Department of Education, United States Catholic Conference, 1979), p. 111.

SOME QUESTIONS FOR REFLECTION AND SHARING

1. If the Church were all that the Spirit of Jesus could enable it to be—what would the Church be like?
   What is Jesus' dream for the Church?
   What is your dream for the Church?
   What is the world's dream for the Church?

2. If the Church were as you envision it to be, what would your parish be like as a local expression of that Church?
   What is Jesus' dream for your parish community?
   What is your dream for your parish community?
   What is your civic community's dream for your parish?

3. If your parish were as you envision it, what would an individual member of your parish community be like?
   What is Jesus' dream for the individual members of your parish?
   What is your dream for the individual members of your parish?
   What is your civic community's dream for the individual members?

4. If every individual member in your parish were as you envisioned, what would your parish community invite you to become?
   What is the Church's dream for you?
   What is Jesus' dream for you?
   What is the dream you hold for yourself as an individual Christian?

5. Try to summarize your earlier responses into a one paragraph "mission statement" for the Church. What is the purpose of the Catholic Church?
   Upon what values does it stand?
   Toward what vision is it moving?

6. Since the Church is a living body, what is needed educationally for the adults of the Church to realize this mission? to live out of these values? to move toward this vision?

7. Try to summarize your earlier responses into a one paragraph "mission statement" for your parish. What is the purpose of your parish community? Upon what values does it stand? Toward what vision is it moving?

8. Looking at your parish's mission statement, what is needed educationally for the adults of your parish to realize this mission?
   What is needed by the parish staff and co-leaders?
   What is needed by the individual membership?

9. Try to summarize your earlier responses into a one paragraph vocation/life-call statement for the baptized adult in your parish community.
   What is the direction or goal of a life-style in Christ?
   What values is an individual Catholic called to live?
   What would be a vision of adult Christian maturation?

Matching Individuals' Needs with Content Areas

In surfacing areas of needs, you will want to think of individuals and groups of adults within your parish, the needs of the parish community as a total body, and the needs of the Church-at-large. For each of these groups, a parish planning committee/staff could brainstorm areas of need and interest. This would be helpful, but if used alone this process would be lacking in validity. You need to involve as many people as possible in the assessment, in the evaluation of the data, in the planning, evaluation, and so on. The last chapter of this workbook contains practical how-to sheets on parish needs assessments. You may wish to refer to these at a later time.

SOME QUESTIONS FOR REFLECTION AND SHARING

1. Working alone or cooperatively with others, try to surface some of the human/religious needs you feel the following groups of people may have. If you are a member of one or more of the following categories, you might reflect back into your own experiences, needs, and interests.

Young Adult Men	Widows and Widowers
Young Adult Women	Grieving Families
Middle Adult Men	Families with Terminally Ill Members
Middle Adult Women	Engaged Couples
Older Adult Men	Gay Men and Lesbian Women
Older Adult Women	Career Persons
Young Married Couples	Retired Persons
Middle-aged Married couples	Unemployed Persons
Older Married Couples	Non-English Speaking Migrants
Young Married Couples with Children	Immigrants
Middle-aged Couples with Teens	Military Personnel and Families
Older Couples with Adult Children	Chemically Dependent Persons
Single Parents with Young Children	Adults in Parish Ministries
Single Parents with Teens	Emotionally Disturbed Persons and Families

Divorced and Separated Singles
Young, Never Married Singles
Middle-aged, Never Married Singles
Older, Never Married Singles

Unchurched and Alienated Persons and Families
Adults Caring for Aged at Home
Handicapped Persons and Families
Families of Mixed Religious Traditions
Infirm Adults
Racial and Ethnic Groups
Hurting Peoples of the Parish
Mobile Persons in the Parish
Other

2. Compare your lists with the life task listings in Chapter II. Are there other things that you would like to add?

3. Compare the preceding groupings with your parish population assessment.
   Which groups will you want to concentrate on first?
   Which groups will you want to place in a holding pattern because they are already being targeted by existing programs, their numbers are small, etc.?

4. Rank order the groups for which you wish to begin program planning.

5. How might you surface the actual needs of this/these groups?
   How might you include them in the planning process?

6. How will your planning proceed?

7. What do you think are some of the needs of the total parish body?
   How might you verify these assumptions?
   How will you involve the parish in this verification?

8. Compare the data from your parish groupings' assessments and your parish-at-large surveys. Are there any similarities?
   Any notable differences?
   Which needs seem most acute at this time?
   Which can be placed in a holding pattern for the future?

9. Compare your results with the following Content Possibility Sheet. Adjust your conclusions if applicable.

Content Possibility Sheet for Adult Religious Education

—Faith sharing/enrichment experiences
—Challenges of Christian community living
—Continuing catechesis—Reconciliation
—Catechesis for marriage
—Christian parenting
—Marriage enrichment
—Social justice
—Biblical concept of stewardship
—Christian decision-making
—Predictable crises in adult life
—Predictable crises in faith
—Challenges of conversion
—Growing through crisis
—Basic teachings of Catholicism/tradition
—Scripture study
—Scriptural prayer
—Study of various topics in theology
—Christian morality
—Church authority
—Christian leadership skills
—Evangelization and you
—Your call to ministry
—Conscience formation
—Role of the Spirit in decision-making
—Human rights issues
—Becoming a self-directed learner
—Communication skills
—Human relations training
—Assertiveness training
—Death, dying, and the paschal mystery
—Various topics—Christian rap groups
—Communicating the faith to the young
—Conflict management
—Interpersonal values/values clarification
—Sexuality
—Christian problem-solving
—Wholistic health
—Christian fitness programs
—Healing of memories
—Living with the elderly at home
—Joys and strains of intergenerational households
—Current problems affecting the family
—Single parent parenting skills
—Doctrine and Christian living
—Christian single life
—Singles issues
—Passages of marriage
—Beginning again—support for widows, widowers
—Singles retreat
—Married retreat

—Family retreat
—Family camp
—Survival skills for divorced and separated
—Sharing groups of various kinds
—Facing death
—Dealing with loneliness
—Growing in intimacy
—Active listening skills
—Parish skills bank
—Christian aspects of work
—Mental health issues
—Coping with physical illness
—Retirement and parish ministry
—Working mothers workshop
—Christian child care
—Roots of ethnic spirituality
—Religious meanings of ethnic customs
—Modern moral problems
—Family dialogue activities
—Christian alternatives in celebrating major holidays
—Family-centered catechesis
—Parish ministry preparation
—Film festivals
—Book clubs
—Social action activities
—Crisis points in marriage
—Christian values in day-to-day living
—Christian business ethics
—Medical ethics/medical decision-making
—Coping with handicapping conditions
—Independent living for the elderly
—Going to college and Christian values
—Shared prayer
—Changes in the Church and you
—Basic introduction to Scripture
—Coping with change
—Growing in self-esteem
—Discussion groups
—Exploring Christian classics
—Charismatic renewal movement
—Cults
—Social plunge experience
—Evenings for families
—Evenings for couples
—Evenings for singles
—Evenings for seniors
—History and the Gospels
—Traditions of the Bible
—Inter-faith discussion/prayer
—Getting the most out of Mass

—Meaning of liturgy
—Crisis and liturgy
—Getting to know you—community days
—Welcome/initiation of new parishioners
—Developing new hobbies/hobby fair
—Meaning and challenge of the kingdom
—Christian spirituality
—Church history and today's teachings/practices
—Family patterns, cycles, passages
—Journal keeping
—Mime and clowning
—Social analysis skills
—Telling your story/personal history review
—Natural family planning
—Christian life-styles
—Challenges of midlife transitions
—Negotiating midlife change
—Discovering your gifts and talents
—Stress management
—Methods of meditation: East and West
—Independent reading and follow-up discussions
  with leader/group on variety of topics
—World religions
—RCIA, baptism, confirmation sponsor enrichment
—Vision of the Church
—Echoing the good news—exploring the Gospels
—Christian discipleship
—Liturgical arts lab
—Liturgical music lab
—Puppets and ministry
—Ministering to the aged
—Ministering to the bereaved
—Ministering to the sick
—Ministering to the dying
—Ministering to the depressed
—Ministering to those in crisis
—Ministering within the family
—Parenting as ministry
—Ministering at work
—Nature/hiking club
—Ministering to those being initiated
—Neighborhood out-reach training

—Meaning of Christian signs and symbols
—Religion and science
—Planning liturgies
—Planning prayer in the home
—Dealing with anger
—Dealing with guilt
—Dealing with depression
—Women's theology/feminist position
—Women in the Church
—History of women in the Church
—Ethnic saints, heroes, heritage days
—Who is Jesus?
—Growth in religious experience
—Meanings of religious feasts
—Storytelling skills
—Ministry of humor
—Christian drama
—Mom's Day Away
—Coping with tots
—Coping with teens
—When they all go to school
—When they all grow up
—Dealing with homosexual orientation
—Parents of children with homosexual orientation
—Community problems
—Families dealing with death
—Welcome home for the alienated
—Christian use of leisure time
—Philosophy—asking life's questions
—Finding meaning in life
—Christian conscience and Church issues
—Getting ready for retirement
—How to personalize Christ in impersonal situations
—Christian theology of recreation
—Current health issues
—Growing in self-understanding
—Political values of liberty and freedom
—Christian views on current issues
—Parish town hall meetings
—Parish forums
—The problem of suffering
—Other

Formal and Informal Adult Religious Education

In a parish, religious education happens formally and informally. Adult religious education happens in-formally in a parish in myriad ways: through the example of leaders, in the ways that resources are used, through its liturgical life, and in the many ways the parishioners serve one another. Adults learn from living religiously and from the many ways a parish community helps them to do so.[6]

Adult religious education happens in formal ways through the parish's adult education programs: study groups, instructional sessions, retreats, ministry training days, faith sharing/prayer groups, films, witnesses, printed materials to be used at home, during homilies, in celebrating sacraments, etc.[7] Service projects with others can also facilitate growth.

Parishes need to assess the needs of and creatively plan for all members. Care must be taken that programs are offered for parish leaders, engaged couples, married couples, parents, singles, widows, widowers, the divorced, the elderly, the handicapped and their families, the sick and grieving people who care for them during terminal illness, career persons, young, middle, and older adults, those with a homosexual orientation, those preparing for a full-time Church ministry and religious vocation, those experiencing a major transition/crisis (unemployment, forced retirement), etc. No single catechetical program will fit the needs and interests of all the members of a parish community. Learning experiences should be designed to help people cope with the issues and religious invitations they are likely to encounter in the styles and stages of their daily lives.

One should not be looking for large numbers. Because adults are problem-centered and already responsible, they should be asked what their interests are and be helped to meet their own needs. This implies many smaller programs rather than fewer larger ones. It necessitates many time frames and learning locations. It means that "how-to" courses and workshops are more likely to succeed than those offered which purely reflect the needs of the institution/instructor. Parishes need to offer more programs which help all different types of groupings to see the connection between their individual human/faith journey and the larger journey of the people of God, between their goals and visions and the larger vision of the kingdom. The process of the RCIA, Scripture study groups, biography sharing times (Christian heroes and heroines, past and present), journal-keeping seminars and follow-up sessions, and faith sharing experiences are a few examples that meet this need. Thomas Groome's praxis method of critical reflection is an excellent methodology with this goal in mind. The method creates space for the sharing of personal experience, image, and story and the exploring of communal myths, images, and doctrines of the Church. The shared praxis method helps adults deepen in awareness of how the tradition weaves itself in and out of their lives, calling forth healing and commitment.[8]

Adult Religious Education and Sacramental Celebration

Adult catechesis offers education for change, including the skills essential for dealing with the rapid changes that are typical today. There is an important relationship between change in life and sacramental events celebrated in the Christian community. The sacraments externalize the relationship between faith growth and maturation in human life. They symbolically announce in word and action the interior movement and external events of the adult life cycle. Catechesis can help adults celebrate the sacraments as rites of passage, helping them through crises and transitions. The sacraments can assist adults in breaking-through the suffering in their lives. The parish community can act as a sacrament of support responding to adults in transition or crisis.[9] Sacramental action/religious ceremony helps adults to examine what they really believe and what they really are experiencing. Catechesis needs to free adults for ritual—formal and deeply personal.[10] Ritual action can be part of adult education experiences, celebrating the places journeyed, the new meaning shared, and the challenges yet to be embraced.

Often adults do not know how to verbalize their needs. A sensitive ear during conversations can help parish leaders tune-in on the life or faith stage needs of those whom they serve. Break times during learning experiences are wonderful opportunities for such listening. Inviting adults to actively sprinkle their thoughts, insights, questions, and concerns over the topic at hand is another such resource.

Learning experiences and liturgical gatherings must begin by affirming the sacred starting places of those present, carefully orchestrating a holy place wherein all can rediscover themselves and the One who walks with them. Program invitations, song and prayer sheets can model the sensitive use of sign/symbol and the word can mold the next stage of growth toward which the learning community is traveling. The tasteful use of banners, greenery, vestments, sculpture, music, and physical movement can also remind the learning community of the deeper meaning at hand.

1. Are the goals of your adult education offerings woven into the liturgical life of the parish?
2. Are the major passages and crises addressed by the liturgical life of the parish?
   Are adults invited to weave their needs and concerns into the parish celebrations?
   Are homilies directed at addressing life issues in the Scriptures and in the lives of the congregation?
3. Do the liturgies actively involve the lives of the congregation with music, symbol, ritual, and ceremony?
4. Is the dynamic of on-going conversion given proper emphasis and application to the challenges of adult life?
5. Have workshops been given developing various aspects of the meaning of the liturgy?
6. Are adults actively involved in liturgical planning and ministries?
7. Is regular training provided for lectors, musicians, cantors, eucharistic ministers, etc.?
8. Are the various ministers of the Eucharist available after service for community building and presence?
9. Are there opportunities to socialize with other parishioners after Mass?
10. Are parishioners actively involved in planning and supporting ministries surrounding funerals, wakes, baptisms, weddings, anointing of the sick, etc.?
11. Is the worship space a suitable, warm, communal environment?
12. Are opportunities provided for intimate, small group/neighborhood liturgies for those who would appreciate them?
13. Are there different levels of involvement/options that parents can take in assisting their children in their preparation for the sacraments?
14. Is there a ministry of welcoming that greets people as they arrive for liturgy and thanks them for their presence? Do priests express their thankfulness to the persons in attendance for liturgy?
15. Is there a feedback system in place where people in the pews can critique or guide the direction of future homilies? Is a dialogue homily done on occasion?
16. Are efforts made to build a small worshiping community with those who attend daily Mass? coffee and donuts afterward? activity in writing petitions? music ministry? option to draw closer to the altar? dialogue homily? faith sharing on readings of the day?
17. Are various opportunities used to catechize on the sacrament of reconciliation and its meaning in negotiating crises, passages, healing of memories, etc?
18. Are efforts made to use the Scriptures during the sacrament of reconciliation as intended in the revised rite?
19. Are liturgies and sacramental celebrations scheduled according to the people's needs rather than the minister's preferences?
20. Are communal celebrations of reconciliation creatively planned, attending to music, ritual, symbols, sufficient ministers, adequate confessional environments, meaningful themes?
21. Are family sacraments of healing developed? Are the skills of forgiveness, reflective listening, peacemaking, reconciliation, etc., addressed, modeled, and encouraged?
22. Does the parish have the new Rite of Adult Initiation and its supporting ministries in place? Is the larger parish community invited to get actively involved in the rites and stages, in the formation and support, in the celebration and follow-up?
23. Are efforts made to involve the newly baptized in parish activities and ministries? Is an adequate mystagogia period in place? Are parishioners involved in the support of this post-baptismal period?

Five Movements Toward Education in the Faith

Since Christian faith is a whole way of being in the world, a lived response rather than a theory about it, adult religious education should invite people to decision. As religious educators, we are called to respond to the workings of God in our lives so that we can move forward in faithfulness toward our individual possibilities and the communal possibility of God's kingdom. A praxis way of knowing calls for critical reflection on one's own experience. Thomas Groome's shared praxis approach in five movements offers us an effective tool in our life's work "to know the Lord."

There are five teaching movements in the shared praxis approach. While the movements are distinct, they are not rigidly separate from each other. They often overlap and are to flow together into a unified experience for the participants.

THE FIVE MOVEMENTS OF CHRISTIAN SHARED PRAXIS[11]

1. First Movement: Present Action (Experience)—Looking at Life

The purpose of the First Movement is to have the learners look at their own life experiences reflective of the session's theme. The experience we invite them to look at may be an everyday experience or it may be their own experience of living and knowing their Christian faith regarding the theme. Inviting the learners to look at their life experiences as indicated by the theme can be done in many creative ways. (Suggestions of adult methodology are found at the end of this book.)

Having brought the learners to encounter the basic human experience of the theme, the First Movement then invites them to express theselves concerning this life experience. Their expression can vary greatly in both content and form. In content, the learners may express what they already know about this theme, or how they feel about it, or how they understand it, or how they live it, or what they believe about it, etc. The forms of their expression can have a great deal of variety as well. The participants can express themselves through words, through activities, through miming, through making something, etc. As long as the learners are brought to express their own experience, their own praxis of the theme, the purpose of the First Movement is being fulfilled.

2. Second Movement: Critical Reflection—Sharing Our Life

The purpose of the Second Movement is to have the adults reflect together on what they have expressed about their own experience in Movement One. It attempts to bring the learners to see the meaning and implications of their own experiences. This Second Movement often invites adults to use their reason in order to understand their experience and to figure out the reasons behind it and the meaning it holds. This movement may also invite the participants to use their memory to recall a particular encounter they have had with this life experience. The Second Movement can often end by inviting the learners to use their imagination. (Notice that memory and imagination as well as reason are all important activities in what is meant here by reflection.)

The first two Movements prepare the adults to encounter God's word and the faith of our Church in the Third Movement. By reflecting on their own experience of the session's theme they are now ready to hear what our people have come to know in faith about this theme over thousands of years of experience and responding to God's activity. But it must be emphasized, however, that Movements One and Two are not just preparatory for Movement Three. These opening Movements must be honored and taken very seriously in their own right. God is making himself known to us, not just in the "faith handed down," but also in the everyday experiences of our own lives.

3. Third Movement: Christian Community Story and Vision—Knowing Our Faith

The purpose of the Third Movement is to make present to the learners the faith of our Christian community concerning the theme of the session. Here, the learners encounter the story of faith that comes to us from our Scripture, tradition, and teaching of the Church, and the faith-life of our people over the ages and in our present time.

The Third Movement also lays out and makes explicit what this Faith means for our lives, and how we are called to live it. In other words, the Third Movement tells our story of faith but it also proposes the vision of our faith, i.e., how we are called to live and respond in faith.

4. *Fourth Movement: Dialectical Hermeneutic Between Story (Tradition) and Story (Individual)—Making the Faith Our Own—Appropriation to Life*

The purpose of the Fourth Movement is to enable the adults to take the faith of the community back to their own life situation, to come to know it for themselves, to make the faith their own. This Fourth Movement helps the learners to appropriate the faith for themselves and to know it as their own. in a real sense, the Fourth Movement places what emerged from the first two Movements into dialogue with what was encountered in the Third Movement.

Sometimes there will be an element of "recall" in the Fourth Movement, when we invite the adults to express what they remember from the Third Movement. But the Fourth Movement is much more than a simple recall of what the teacher has taught. It also invites the learners to come to see for themselves what our faith means for their lives. The Fourth Movement appeals not only to their heads, but to their hearts and lifestyles as well.

5. *Fifth Movement: Dialectical Hermeneutic Between the Vision (Kingdom of God) and our Vision—Living Our Faith, Decision, Response*

The purpose of the Fifth Movement is, by God's grace, to bring the adults to a lived faith response. In his preaching and life, Jesus always invited a lived faith response from his hearers. Our faith is not yet a "living faith" until we live it out in our lives. By inviting the learners to decision, the Fifth Movement is intended to bring the adults to a response of "living our faith."

Our faith is what we believe, but it is also much more than what we claim to believe. Faith is our whole relationship with God in Jesus Christ and the concrete actions we take to live out our faith in our daily lives. Because we understand Christian faith as a whole way of life that engages our heads, hearts and lifestyles, the faith response invited in the Fifth Movement can take a variety of different expressions. The Fifth Movement may invite a response of prayer and praise to God, sometimes set in a communal prayer celebration. The Fifth Movement may invite the adults to a concrete decision for action, a decision about how to live their Christian faith. The session that began with their own lived situations has now returned to those situations again with a decision and response for living our faith.

> **Note:** For further reading concerning Tom Groome's shared praxis methodology, read: *Christian Religious Education: Sharing Our Story and Vision.* San Francisco: Harper and Row, Publishers, 1980.

SOME QUESTIONS FOR REFLECTION AND SHARING

1. Look at the following definitions or statements about faith. Mark the ones that you agree with or appear valid when compared with your own life experience.[12]

   a. Faith is a form of trust.
   b. Faith is a kind of obedience.
   c. Faith is the power to overcome obstacles.
   d. Faith is a dedication to a certain way of life.
   e. Faith is accepting the unknown.
   f. Faith is a relationship.
   g. Faith is a way of looking at life.
   h. Faith makes life difficult.
   i. Faith is obedience to religious leaders.
   j. Faith means keeping the commandments.
   k. Faith is belief in a set of doctrines.
   l. Faith allows questioning and doubt.
   m. Faith means helping others spiritually.

n. Faith is mainly concerned with life after death.
o. Faith means being at peace.
p. Faith is mainly a matter of feeling.
q. Faith is mainly a matter of knowing.
r. Faith means I have been forgiven.
s. Faith means helping others in their worldly needs.
t. Faith involves belonging to a community of believers.
u. Faith is a search for meaning.
v. Faith is caring for yourself.
w. Faith is a struggle against unbelief.
x. Faith is an effort to see God in daily life.
y. Faith is openness to the activity of conversion.
z. Faith is a life stance that is both human and religious.

2. Why did you select the statements you did? Why did you reject the statements you did? What do you think is the Catholic definition of faith? Would that definition be shared by other churches? Explain.

3. Write a definition of faith as you understand and live it. Have you always understood faith in this way? If your understanding has changed, name the factors that have influenced such a movement. What has supported this faith in your parish community? What supports do you wish were present?

4. If religious education is education in faith, what would you see as the necessary components of a methodology/process of faith education? Explain.

5. How would your process differ from Tom Groome's Christian Shared Praxis? How is it similar? What does Shared Christian Praxis challenge in your own religious education practice? What does it support? Explain.

6. Can you see any connections between a shared praxis approach in religious education and stages of adult growth and development? Do you think a shared praxis approach is valid as a method in moving adults toward Christian maturity? Explain.

Summary

Adult religious education/catechesis confronts the faith community and individual adults with the kingdom of God. Adult learning enables Christians to concretely respond to the needs and problems of our Church and world in a way that is rooted in the Church's experience of the life, death, and resurrection of Jesus. The process of adult learning empowers the individual Christian adult and the faith community of the parish. Good adult religious education calls forth and enables the gifts of each adult for the common good. As adult catechesis enables learners to discover God's activity in their midst it enables the faith community to see God's vision and possibilities. Adults who learn become the faith community's resource for mission and ministry.

Adult catechesis respects and responds to the developmental nature of the adult learner. It acknowledges the needs of individuals and attempts to provide support and resources on the cognitive, affective, and reflective levels. In doing so, catechesis respects the diversity of values, customs, spiritualities, cultures, etc., within the learning community and uses it to maximize insights and foster unity.

The adult learning community must be an environment of hospitality and Christian outreach. It should provide support and opportunities for spiritual growth. The learning community needs to be a place where the kingdom is recognizable, where healing takes place, where new freedom is tried out, where liberation is possible. The responsibility for creating such an environment is shared by all. The facilitator needs to model or witness the message and the vision in all aspects of the learning experience. More adult learning happens by being Church than by teaching about it!

Catechesis reminds "the redeemed community that it is never quite redeemed; its members are never perfectly whole. We lapse, we waver, we are intimidated, we lose confidence, we break trust, we cover up our real needs, we negotiate, we manipulate, we justify . . . and we need to be forgiven, summoned again by the liturgical word and reconstituted by a giving, graceful body of mutually caring persons around the banquet table of Christ. We always need re-membering."[13] It reminds us that we are larger than our story, that we are always in process, that we are always moving with the Lord into adulthood.

CHAPTER V

Techniques for Effective Adult Education

Possibilities in Educational Techniques and Devices[1]

What is the **best** technique? There is no answer to this question. It depends on your PURPOSE. Technique may be classified by purpose, although a particular technique may have usefulness for other purposes as well. Some techniques impart knowledge. Others teach a skill. Some techniques are used to change attitudes. Others encourage creativity.

Most techniques are best used in combination with other techniques. Many techniques require other particular techniques as follow-ups. What is the worst technique? The one that is used all the time, whatever it is! Variety is the spice of life and adds to the success of a meaningful catechetical experience.

Instructional Techniques To Impart Knowledge[2]

Techniques appropriate for *One Resource Person Presentations* to inform, give information, disseminate knowledge, develop understanding:

Committee Hearing	Questioning of a resource person by a panel of interviewers for extemporaneous responses	

| **Film** | One-way organized presentation | |

| **Interview** | Questioning of a resource person by an individual on behalf of an audience | |

| **Lecture, Speech** | One-way organized formal presentation of information or point of view by resource person | |

| **Lecture with Group Response Team (Audience Reaction Team)** | Several group representatives interrupt resource person at appropriate times for immediate clarification of issues | |

| **Screened Speech** | Sub-groups develop questions they wish resource person to address extemporaneously | |

Techniques appropriate for *Several Resource Person Presentations* to inform, give information, disseminate knowledge, develop understanding:

Colloquy	Panels of 3 or 4 resource persons and 3 or 4 representatives of the audience discussing issue	
Debate	Conflicting views stated by each resource person and clarified further by argument between them	
Dialog	Informal, conversational discourse between 2 resource persons	
Dramatic Presentation	Prepared play or skit to inform	
Interrogator Panel	2 to 4 resource persons questions by 2 to 4 interrogators	

| **Panel Discussion** | Panel of 4 to 7 resource persons carry on a discussion of an issue before an audience (informal discussion "overheard" by audience) |  |

| **Symposium** | 3 to 6 speeches or lectures presented in turn by resource persons on various phases of a single subject or problem | 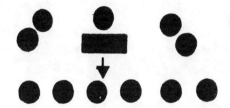 |

Techniques appropriate as *Follow-ups* to presentations of one or more resource persons to involve the audience:

| **Buzz Groups** | Sub-groups of 4 to 6, with 4 to 6 minutes to discuss particular issue or question raised by resource person. | 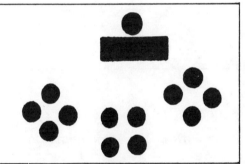 |

| **Chain Reaction Forum** | Sub-groups discuss presentation and formulate questions to be asked resource person. | 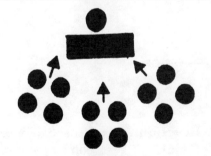 |

| **Forum** | Free and open question/discussion period immediately following a lecture. | 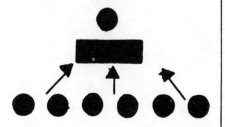 |

Group Discussion	Sub-groups of 10-20 discuss problems or issues raised, for 15-30 minutes.	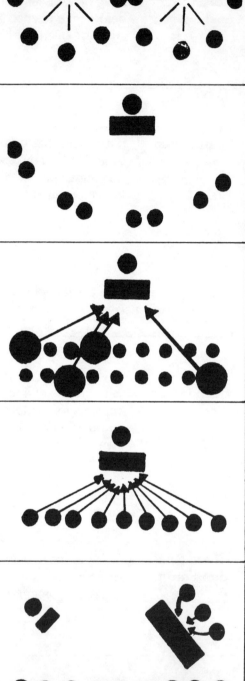
Huddle Groups	Pairs or triads (2-3 persons/groups) discuss specific issue for 2 to 3 minutes.	
Listening Team	3-4 members in audience are designated to listen and raise questions after presentation.	
Question Period	Opportunity for any in audience to directly question speaker.	
Reaction Panel	Panel of 3 or 4 react to presentation by panel discussion.	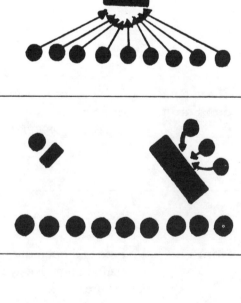

Reaction Symposium	3 or 4 persons in turn give their reaction to presentation
Screening Panel	3 or 4 persons screen questions raised by audience (on cards) before presenting questions to resource person.

Instructional Techniques To Teach a Skill[3]

TECHNIQUES APPROPRIATE TO TEACH A SKILL OR CHANGE A BEHAVIOR:	
Techniques	*Description*
Case Study	Presentation of a problem or case for a small group to analyze and solve.
Demonstration	Instructor verbally explains and performs an act, procedure or process.
Games, Structured Experiences	Under leadership of instructor, learners participate in a "game" requiring particular skills.
Simulation	Learners learn skills in a setting that simulates the real setting where skills are required.
Teaching/ Learning Team	Working cooperatively, small groups of 3–6 persons each teach and help each other develop skills.

TECHNIQUES APPROPRIATE FOR FOLLOW-UP AND PRACTICE OF SKILLS:	
Technique	*Description*
Application Projects	Performance contracts, check lists, specific exercises to apply learnings "back home."
Drill	Practice beyond the point needed for recall to produce automatic response.
Practice	Repeated performance of a skill under supervision of instructor, and then without supervision.

Instructional Techniques To Change Attitudes[4]

Attitudes are most likely to be changed in a context of free and open discussion, in a climate of trust. In such a climate, assumptions and attitudes can be examined with less threat and defensive behavior.

TECHNIQUES APPROPRIATE TO CHANGE ATTITUDES, VALUES, OPINIONS, FEELINGS:	
Technique	*Description*
Circle Response	Question posed to members of a group seated in a circle, each person in turn expressing a response.
Exercises, Structured Experiences	Planned activities in which learners participate, after which they discuss feelings and reactions.
Field Trips, Tours	Experiencing or viewing actual situations for first hand observation and study.
Games	Experiencing a game and discussing its application to real life.
Group Discussion	Circle face to face mutual exchange of ideas and opinions by members of small groups (8–20) on problem or issue of mutual concern for 10–40 minutes, depending on size of group.
Process Group (T-Groups, Laboratory Groups)	Circle of 8–12 people studying themselves in process of becoming and being a group.
Role Playing	Impromptu dramatization of a problem or situation, followed by discussion.
Sensitivity Group	Circle of 8–12 people helping each other through self-disclosure and feedback.
Simulation	Experience in a situation as near real as possible, followed by discussion.
Skit	Short rehearsed dramatic presentation, followed by discussion.
Values Clarification	Structured experiences designed to help learner examine values held.

Virtually every technique listed above requires *Process Time*, opportunity for learners to evaluate, discuss, and process the experience.

TECHNIQUES APPROPRIATE TO ENCOURAGE CREATIVITY, NEW IDEAS, THINKING IN NEW PATHS:	
Technique	*Description*
Brainstorming (ideation: idea inventory)	Free flowing and uninhibited sharing and listing of ideas by a group without evaluation or consideration of practicality; object is to generate as many creative ideas as possible.
Nominal Group Process (Delbecq Technique)	A specific procedure for a group of 5–8 people for maximum idea generation and narrowing the range of ideas: 1. Each person makes his own list of ideas (5–10 minutes) 2. Master list is made on newsprint in round robin fashion as each contributes one idea to list until all ideas are on master list (10–15 minutes) 3. Clarification (but not discussion) of items on master list (15 minutes) 4. Each person chooses 5 items from the master list without discussion (5 minutes) 5. Each person ranks 5 items and accords value points (5 for first, 4 for second, 3 for third, 2 for fourth, 1 for fifth) 6. "Votes" (value points) are recorded for each item on master list. 7. Ideas receiving the most points are discussed.
Quiet Meeting (Quaker Meeting)	15–60 minute period of reflection and limited verbal expression by group members; periods of silence and spontaneous verbal contributions.
Self-analysis and Reflection	Time allocated for personal reflection and opportunity to relax and examine learning alone.

N.B. The graphics and text on the preceding pages of this chapter are taken almost entirely from: Russell D. Robinson, *An Introduction to Helping Adults Learn and Change*, (Mulwake, WI: Omnibook Co., 1979), pp. 89–95.

Methods for Individual Learning[6]

Method	*Description*
Apprenticeship	Under the guidance of experienced worker
Computer-assisted Instruction	Interaction with programmed computer
Correspondence Study	Course by mail; reading with the guidance of a syllabus, written assignments reviewed and reacted to by an instructor
Counseling	Help from a counselor geared toward self-insight
Directed Individual Study	Tailor-made reading sequences to help individuals engage in self-directed inquiry

Method	Description
Field Experience	Supervised field work
Independent Reading/Study	Learner-initiated systematic reading/study
Individual Learning Project	Learner-initiated uses of resources to accomplish specific learning
Observation/Imitation	Observing and imitating another's performance
Programmed Learning Materials Teaching Machines	Course outlined step by step, with immediate feedback on learning; branches for reinforcement
Supervision	Help from supervisor
Tutorial/Coaching	One-on-one with instructor
Multimedia Learning Packages	Sequences of learning experiences made up of a combination of printed materials, diagnostic instruments, audiotapes, films, slide films, microfiche, exercises, workbooks, evaluation instruments, etc.

Methods for Small Group Learning (up to 30)[7]

Method	Description
Class/Course	Series over a period of time
Clinic	Diagnosis, analysis, and solving problems
Clubs/Organized Groups	In almost every club one purpose is the education of its members
Colloquium	An advanced group where research projects are planned and evaluated as they progress
Committee	3–7 members with a specific task(s)
Discussion Group	8–15 members discussing mutually agreed concerns and issued usually with the assistance of a discussion leader
Executive Committee/Board	5–9 members with general overseeing responsibilities
Laboratory Group	8–15 studying their own group processes, usually with trainer or facilitator
Residential Learning	Live-in experience of several days
Round Table	Intensive analysis of a specific problem(s) common to all present

Method	Description
Seminar	Advanced students in specialized study, learning from discussing their projects and experience with each other
Sensitivity Group	8–15 helping each other through self-disclosure and feedback, usually with trainer
Short Course	Abbreviated versions of longer courses, tailored to clientele
Training Session	Specific skill-building focus
Task Force	Seeking a specific answer or specified result
Workshop	Emphasis on work sessions, problem-solving, output
Action Projects	Improving skills as agents of change; increase knowledge about problem on which taking action
Demonstration	Organized to participate in demonstration as experimenters or observers; shown how to do it followed by time for individual practice
Trips/Tours/Studycades	Reading list, discussion, identifying questions, tour/trip, consolidating learning

Methods for Large Group/Mass Learning (more than 30)[8]

Method	Description
Assembly	Usually for purpose of agreement on some action
Conference	One or more days to consider topics using a variety of techniques
Forum	Usually presentation of information followed by audience questions and participation
Institute	Concentrated sessions, usually over several days for development of knowledge or skills in a specialized area
Lecture Series	A lecture course with same or different speakers over a period of time
Large Meeting	One-to-three hour sessions
Orientation Sessions	To provide information to a new group
Work Conference	Working on problems rather than considering topics

Method	Description
Congress/Convention	Several days with total group and smaller group sessions bringing together local members in a district, state, or national meeting
Community Action Groups	For the purpose of taking action in the community
Community Problem-Solving Groups	For the purpose of solving problems
Community Development Groups	A process involving the community in its own development and improvement
Community Project Groups	For the purpose of accomplishing a project
Exhibit, Fair, Festival	For the purpose of displaying wares, accomplishments, demonstrations of the above, etc.
Result Demonstration	For the purpose of displaying results

Various Purposes for Small Groups in Adult Learning[9]

Group	Description
Topical Discussion Groups	Organized for the purpose of reacting to, testing the meaning of, or sharing ideas about informational inputs from reading or speakers on given topics
Laboratory Groups	Organized for the purpose of analysizing group behavior, experimenting with new behavior, and sharing feedback regarding the effects of various behaviors
Special-Interest Groups	Organized according to categories of interest of participants for the purpose of sharing experiences and exploring common concerns
Problem-Solving Groups	Organized to develop solutions to procedural or substantive problems of concern to the total assembly
Planning Groups	Organized to develop plans for activities within the design or for back-home applications
Instructional Groups	Organized to receive instruction through the services of resource experts in specialized areas of knowledge, understanding, or skill
Inquiry Groups	Organized to search out information and report their findings to the total assembly

Method	Description
Evaluation Groups	Organized for the purpose of developing proposals for evaluating results of the activity for the approval of the entire assembly; perhaps executing the approved plans
Skill Practice Groups	Organized for the purpose of practicing specified categories of skills
Consultative Groups	Organized for the purpose of giving consultation to one another
Operational Groups	Organized for the purpose of carrying responsibilities for the operation of the activity, such as room arrangements, refreshments, materials preparation, equipment operation, etc.
Learning-Teaching Teams	Groups which take responsibility for learning all they can about a content unit and sharing what they have learned with the total assembly
Dyads	Two person groups organized to share experiences, coach each other, plan strategies, or help each other in any other way
Triads	Three-person group organized for mutually helpful purposes
Buzz Groups	Randomly organized groups of three or four persons that meet in a general assembly to pool problems, ideas, reactions, and report them through a spokesman to the assembly

N.B. The text of these pages is also taken almost entirely from: Russell D. Robinson, *An Introduction to Helping Adults Learn and Change* (Mulwake, WI: Omnibook, Co., 1979), pp. 70–72, aside from the final section, which is taken directly from: Malcolm Knowles, *The Modern Practice of Adult Education: From Pedagogy to Andragogy* (Chicago: Follett Publishing Company, 1980), pp. 236–237.

Types of Teaching Activities[10–11]

Verbal Activities have been the most common means used in teaching. Teaching activities in this category are: lecture, discussion, recording, homily, story, reading, and any other type of verbal presentation that depends primarily upon the hearing of the learner. The evidence is that most people do not learn well just by hearing something. In order to be effective, verbal activities must be accompanied by other types of experiences. Hearing for most persons is a passive activity not requiring much participation from the learner. Also, hearing is very selective. We tend to hear what we want to hear.

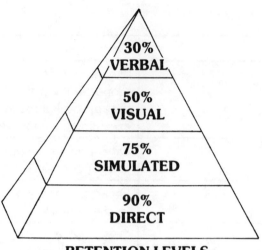

**RETENTION LEVELS
OF VARIOUS LEARNING METHODS**

Another category of teaching activities is the use of visual symbols. **Visual Symbols** involve the learners through their sense of seeing. Activities in this category are: use of teaching pictures, filmstrips, map study, seeing movies, looking at books, and many other types of visual presentations. Most persons learn more from what they see than from what they hear. Seeing is less passive than hearing. Seeing elicits a response from the one who sees. When verbal and visual symbols are used together in a combined activity, the learning is more effective than when either is used separately.

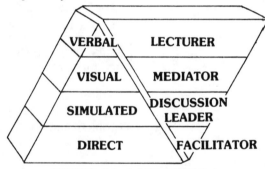

**TYPES OF ACTIVITIES
ROLES OF TEACHER AND LEARNERS**

Simulated Experiences move us a step farther than verbal and visual activities. To simulate is to act out, to act as if it is real but it is not actually real. Teaching activities in this category are role playing, dramatics, simulation games, some field trips, some creative writing and other experiences which place learners in positions of acting out particular feelings, problems, or issues. A simulation activity involves the learners more significantly in developing and identifying with the concepts of the learning experience.

Direct Experiences are those activities when learners are actually involved in "for real" situations, problems, and concepts.

The more our learning activities are in the direction of verbal symbols the less involved the learners are and the less they will learn. The more our teaching moves toward direct and simulated experiences the more the learners will be involved in their own learning. Teaching activities at a verbal level tend to restrict the participation and learning of many adults, whereas teaching activities involving direct experiences tend to include all the learners in one way or another.

Graphics taken from: Mary K. Cove, SSJ and Jane E. Regan, *TREP: Teaching Religion Effectively Program* (Dubuque, Iowa: Wm. C. Brown Publishers, 1982), pp. 29 and 31. **Text taken from:** Donald L. Griggs, *Teaching Teachers To Teach* (Nashville: Abingdon Press, 1974), pp. 17–22.

Resources for Learning Activities[12]

Learning activities are what leaders and learners do in a session to experience and communicate particular concepts. RESOURCES are what teachers/leaders/facilitators USE in the process of teaching and learning.

RESOURCES FOR VERBAL ACTIVITIES

—audio-tapes
—records
—recording and playback devices
—resource books without diagrams, maps or photos; just words
—pens, pencils and writing paper for writing activities

RESOURCES FOR VISUAL ACTIVITIES

—maps, charts, posters, photographs, banners
—filmstrips and projectors
—overhead projector and transparencies
—16mm films and projectors
—8mm cameras, films and projectors
—chalk board, bulletin board, white board
—books with photographs, paintings, diagrams
—magazine pictures, maps
—35mm cameras, slides, projectors
—write-on slides, filmstrips, and films
—information briefs
—summaries
—hand-outs
—study guides

—publications
—books and pamphlets
—newspapers
—magazines
—video-tapes, television
—articles
—annotated reading lists
—charts
—posters
—drawings
—cork boards
—flipcharts
—hook and loop boards
—opaque projector, opaque projection

RESOURCES FOR SIMULATED ACTIVITIES

—directions and supplies for simulation games
—scripts, props, costumes for drama
—materials for constructing models
—structured experiences
—discussion starters, discussion guides

—puppetry
—skits, plays, mime
—in-basket exercises
—critical incidents
—case studies
—stem completions

RESOURCES FOR DIRECT EXPERIENCE ACTIVITIES

—all of the above resources could be used to help learners do something directly related to the key concept that is connected with their own life experiences
—service projects, urban plunge, social analysis activities, community action projects

Lincoln Christian College

Room Arrangements[13]

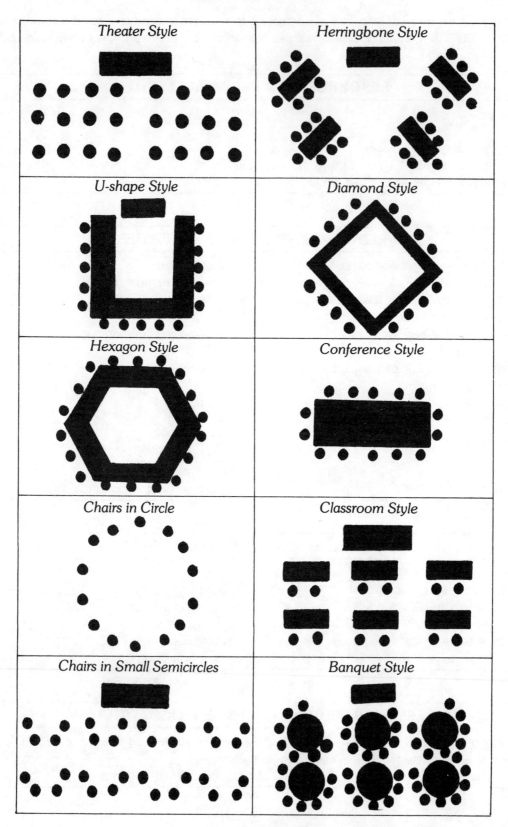

Taken from: Russell D. Robinson, *An Introduction to Helping Adults Learn and Change* (Mulwake, WI: Omnibook, Co., 1979), p. 97.

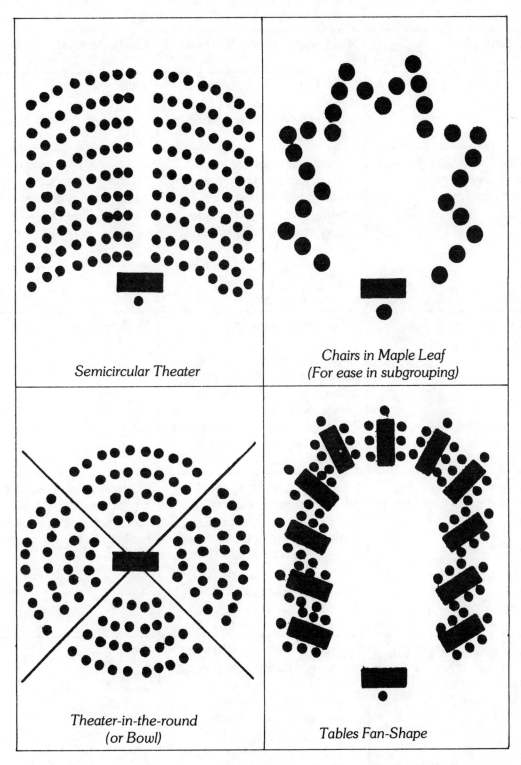

Semicircular Theater

Chairs in Maple Leaf
(For ease in subgrouping)

Theater-in-the-round
(or Bowl)

Tables Fan-Shape

Taken from: Malcolm Knowles, *The Modern Practice of Adult Education: From Pedagogy to Andragogy* (Chicago: Follett Publishing Company, 1980), pp. 164–165.

Most Effective Methods for Basic Types of Learning[15]

Type of Educational Objective	Most Appropriate Methods	Usefulness of Groups
Community Building	Serendipity, games sharing common tasks, shared projects, liturgical celebrations, shared reflection/prayer	High
Knowledge (Absorbing facts and generalizations about experience with some internalization of information)	Lecture, television, debate, dialogue, interview, symposium, panel, group interview, colloquy, motion pictures, slide film, recording, book-based discussion, reading, programmed instruction, field trips, exhibits, recitation, research projects	Low: Group process most helpful in processing information and making it one's own
Understanding (Application of information and generalizations)	Audience participation, demonstration, Socratic discussion, problem-solving project, case method, critical incident process, simulation games, problem-solving discussion, team inquiry project, writing assignments, laboratory group analysis	Moderate
Skills (Incorporating new ways of performing through practice)	Skill practice exercise, role-playing, in-basket exercises, participative cases, simulation games, human relations training groups, non-verbal exercises, drilling, coaching, laboratory experimentation, discussion practice, participant-observation, practice teaching	Moderate: unless skills involved are group skills which require coordination and cooperation. Individuals can learn from one another
Attitudes (Adoption of new feelings through experiencing greater success with them than with old feelings)	Experience-sharing discussion, sensitivity training, role-playing, critical-incident process, case method, simulation games, participative cases, group therapy, counseling, role reversal, permissive discussion, feedback laboratory groups, field trips, intercultural collaborative projects	High

Type of Educational Objective	Most Appropriate Methods	Usefulness of Groups
Values (the adoption and priority arrangements of beliefs)	Value-clarification exercises, biographical reading, lecture, debate, symposium, colloquy, dramatization, role-playing, critical-incident process, simulation games, sensitivity training, sermons, visits with great personalities	High
Development of Interests	Satisfying exposure to new interests: field trips, exhibits, demonstrations, assignments, group projects	High

Taken from: Diocese of Youngstown, *Aspirgrow Consultant Training Handbook* (Youngstown: Diocese of Youngstown, 1978), p. 4.0.

Matching Techniques to Desired Behavioral Outcomes[16]

TYPE OF BEHAVIORAL OUTCOME	MOST APPROPRIATE TECHNIQUES
KNOWLEDGE (Generalizations about experience; internalization of information)	Lecture, television, debate, dialog, interview, symposium, panel, group interview, colloquy, motion picture, slide film, recording, book-based discussion, reading.
UNDERSTANDING (Application of information and generalizations)	Audience participation, demonstration, motion picture, dramatization, socratic discussion, problem-solving discussion, case discussion, critical incident process, case method, games.
SKILLS (Incorporation of new ways of performing through practice)	Role playing, in-basket exercise, games, action mazes, participative cases, T-Group, nonverbal exercises, skill practice exercises, drill, coaching.
ATTITUDES (Adoption of new feelings through experiencing greater success with them than with old)	Experience-sharing discussion, group-centered discussion, role playing, critical incident process, case method, games, participative cases, T-Group, nonverbal exercises.

TYPE OF BEHAVIORAL OUTCOME	MOST APPROPRIATE TECHNIQUES
VALUES (The adoption and priority arrangement of beliefs)	Television, lecture (sermon), debate, dialog, symposium, colloquy, motion picture, dramatization, guided discussion, experience-sharing discussion, role playing, critical incident process, games, T-group.
INTERESTS (Satisfying exposure to new activities)	Television, demonstration, motion picture, slide film, dramatization, experience-sharing discussion, exhibits, trips, nonverbal exercises.

Taken from: Malcolm S. Knowles, *The Modern Practice of Adult Education: From Pedagogy to Andragogy* (Chicago: Follett Publishing Company, 1980), p. 240.

Learning Style Inventory[17]

This inventory is designed to assess your method of learning. As you take the inventory, give a high rank to those words which best characterize the way you learn and a low rank to the words which are least characteristic of your learning style.

You may find it hard to choose the words that best describe your learning style because there are no right and wrong answers.

Different characteristics described in the inventory are equally good. The aim of the inventory is to describe *how you learn*, not to evaluate your learning ability.

Instructions

There are nine sets of four words listed below. Rank in order, each set of four words, assigning a 4 to the word which best characterizes your learning style, a 3 to the word which next best characterizes your learning style, a 2 to the next most characteristic word, and a 1 to the word which is least characteristic of you as a learner. Be sure to assign a different rank number to each of the words in each set. Do not make ties.

I	II	III	IV
1) __ discriminating	1) __ tentative	1) __ involved	1) __ practical
2) __ receptive	2) __ relevant	2) __ analytical (break down whole to understand parts)	2) __ impartial
3) __ feeling	3) __ watching	3) __ thinking	3) __ doing
4) __ accepting	4) __ risk-taking	4) __ evaluative	4) __ aware
5) __ intuitive (known without conscious use of reason)	5) __ productive	5) __ logical	5) __ questioning
6) __ abstract	6) __ observing	6) __ concrete	6) __ active
7) __ present-oriented	7) __ reflecting	7) __ future-oriented	7) __ pragmatic (practical)
8) __ experience	8) __ observation	8) __ conceptualization	8) __ experimentation
9) __ intense	9) __ reserved	9) __ rational	9) __ responsible

Directions for scoring:

Now add up the numerical sum of the ranking numbers you gave to the question numbers indicated in column I. This will give you your CE score. Proceed to column II. Add up the ranking numbers of the questions listed below. This will give you your RO score. Continue the same ways for columns III and IV giving you your AC and AE scores.

CE _____ RO _____ AC _____ AE _____
2,3,4,5,7,8   1,3,6,7,8,9   2,3,4,5,8,9   1,3,6,7,8,9

Learning Style Inventory Plotting Sheet[18]

Directions: Take your CE score and plot it along the CE line. Start at the center, O, and move along until you can mark in your actual CE score. Do the same for your RO, AC, and AE scores.

Connect your four plotting points, making a four-sided figure. Note which quadrants are larger and which are smaller. The dominant areas of your figure indicate your preferred style(s) of learning.

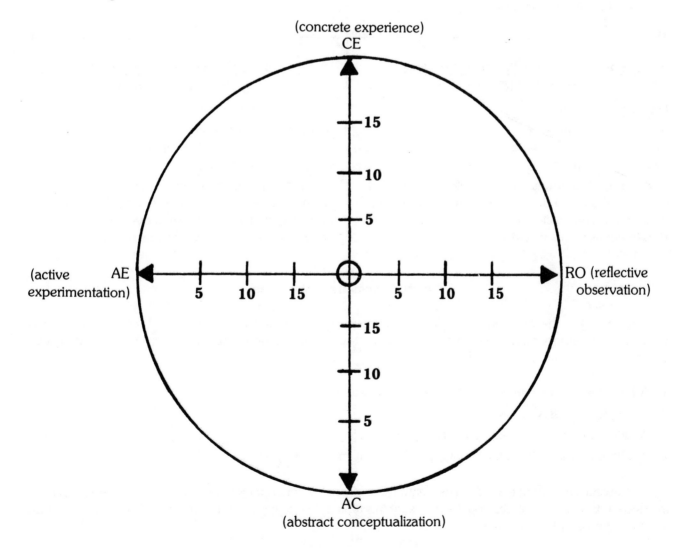

Interpreting the Learning Styles Plotting Sheet[19–21]

The dominant area(s) on your circle chart indicate the way(s) you prefer to process concepts into meaning. All learners fall somewhere on this plotting sheet. In any learning situation, it is likely that most if not all learning styles will be present.

If you are using this inventory with others, it might be interesting and helpful to share individual results noting similarities and differences. Compare your preferred style(s) of learning with the way(s) you like to teach. Most people teach the way they prefer to learn.

Adult educators must plan for the learning styles of all members in the group and not just their own.

IV. ACTIVE EXPERIENCE LEARNING PREFERENCE

General Characteristics:

practical   active
doing   experimentation
pragmatic   responsible

Summary: AE learners will listen until they get the gist of a presentation and then make intuitive leaps on their own. They "catch on" quickly. AE learners prefer to work alone. "Trial and error" is their favorite style of learning.

I. CONCRETE EXPERIENCE LEARNING PREFERENCE

General Characteristics:

receptive   accepting
feeling   present-oriented
intuitive   experiential

Summary: CE learners prefer concrete presentations. They need black and white learning experiences, step by step directions, and hands-on activities.

III. ABSTRACT CONCEPTUALIZATION LEARNING PREFERENCE

General Characteristics:

analytical   evaluative
thinking   conceptualization
logical   rational

Summary: AC learners automatically decode written and spoken data into symbols. They create their own mental pictures and enjoy well-organized presentations with substance.

II. REFLECTIVE OBSERVATION LEARNING PREFERENCE

General Characteristics:

tentative   observing
watching   observation-oriented
reflecting   reserved

Summary: RO learners enjoy meetings, discussions, and an unstructured receiving of information. They like to mull over or reflect upon concepts and then draw conclusions.

Needs Assessment Vehicles

According to the research the basic adult learning styles are related to specific and discernible patterns. One of the foremost researchers in this area of pattern identification comes from Dr. Donnie Dutton who notes:[22]

1. Adults learn best when they have a strong desire to learn.
2. Adults learn best when they have clear goals.
3. Adults learn best when they put forth an effort to learn.
4. Adults learn best when they receive satisfaction from what they learn.

It becomes apparent that adults will learn most effectively when they themselves are directly and actively involved in the process of learning. Of necessity this type of learning pattern excludes the "come and hear me lecture" approach toward adult education.

One of the primary purposes of adult learning is to effect change. Far too many program planners overlook the need for creative and varied adult educational activities. One approach to program planning is to follow a simple guide in the planning process itself. There are four key areas where program planners need to take stock. The following check list may be of benefit for planners:

A Checklist: Questions To Ask Before Planning a Program[23]

What is the purpose of this program?

Personnel: 1) Who are the learners and teachers in this program and what are their competencies?
               2) How shall the learners and teachers interact in this program?

Scope: 1) What is the appropriate scope for a program of religious education?
               2) What are the themes for this program?
               3) Are we trying to cover too much territory and consequently are not specific in our appeal?

Process: 1) How do we expect people to learn in this program?
               2) What is our motivation for learning in this program?
               3) What are the learning tools needed for this type of program?
               4) What are our expectations for this program?

Context: 1) Where and under what circumstances will this program take place?
               2) How shall the learning session be constructed?
               3) What is the quality of the spatial and social environment in which this learning program will take place?

Some Challenges Facing Today's Parish Planners

◇ one out of five families are single parent families with a projection that nearly 40% will be in the future

◇ nearly ½ of all marriages involve Catholic/non-Catholic spouses

◇ less than ¼ of all children in Catholic families are enrolled in Catholic schools

◇ there is a stronger influence in the lives of families because of TV and outside-the-home factors than existed prior to 1960

◇ families are not automatically supportive of parish staff

◇ 75% of mothers of children between 6–17 work at least part-time

◇ there is an increase of Catholics who "shop around" for a parish as opposed to geographical parishioners with strong local ties and identities

◇ families have surrendered many of their natural functions to institutions

◇ there are fewer children per family today than 20 years ago

◇ there has been a rapid increase in the "retirement age" population

◇ there are currently 49 million active Catholics and 12 million estranged Catholics

◇ one of the primary causes for estrangement from Catholicism is cited as the deterioration of Catholic family life and the inability to pass on Catholic values to children

◇ ineffective preaching and the poor quality of Catholic worship are cited as contributing factors to disillusionment among Catholics

◇ many Catholic adults are still unable to distinguish between essential teachings which do not change and accidental teachings which do change

◇ unresolved controversy over such issues as birth control, ordination of women, marriage after divorce, intercommunion and democratization of the Church

Adapted from: Patrick Brennan, "Recycling and Reentering the Church: Evangelization and Lapsed Catholics," *Christian Initiation Resources*, Vol. 1 (Wm. Sadlier Inc., N.Y., 1981), pp. 6–9.

A Fact Sheet on Publicity

◇ Most successful publicity depends on personnel who are articulate, enthusiastic, creative, and persuasive. It doesn't hurt to have someone who can type or use duplicating equipment.

◇ Every group should have a chairperson, two committee people, a task force or subcommittee to handle specific responsibilities and a co-chairperson.

◇ Some good methods for obtaining broad positive coverage of a program include:

–Local bulletins with easily identifiable logo or heading
–New releases for radio, TV and newspapers
–Calendars both local and city wide
–Personal contacts (50% of your audience will be there because of a personal invitation or endorsement of a friend)
–Direct mailings to parishioners with enclosed leaflets, calendars, etc.
–Handouts at church on cars
–Posters or visual aids for parish and local church facilities
–Local endorsements from area colleges and schools printed on flyers

◇ Publicity is telling the people your story. Be sure to include who is the group sponsoring the activity, what is being offered, when and by whom.

◇ Publicity expenses are a major part of a successful program. Be sure to budget for them accordingly. A good rule of thumb is to allow at least 10% of the total program cost for publicity.

◇ Don't ever be afraid to sponsor a program which will not be a "money maker." An investment in the adult educational growth of a parish community is a sound and prudent use of parishioner donations.

◇ Believe in yourself, your team and your vision. It takes a measure of courage to chart new courses and try new ideas. Adult learning is an experience upon which an entire Church can build. Take the risk to make it happen.

Today

Adults are people who:[24]

◇ have a large number of experiences available to them. Some reflect and grow; others don't and won't.

◇ are pretty set in their ways: attitudes, responses, defenses, life styles, tastes. They need "space" to exercise options freely.

◇ could really enjoy interdependence, if their personal and community history didn't put them under the tyranny of "should": so in some ways they are independent; in others, dependent.

◇ risk more serious loss than young people. An opportunity taken and muffed can mean personal disaster.

◇ seldom think of themselves as an "authority" and so rarely have the pleasurable experience of their own energy flow.

◇ need to resolve problems which can't be left at home during a learning experience.

◇ crave entertainment/relaxation. And deserve it!

◇ are faced with more options than in their previous lifestyle.

◇ exercise a repertoire of defense mechanisms in group or one-on one.

◇ like other people, need to feel safe. Change in values, attitudes, emotional responses are difficult. They require support and commitment.

◇ hear what they want—or can't help hearing!

◇ come alive with real affirmation.

◇ fear losing control or getting old.

◇ don't start at ground zero: they have knowledge to share.

◇ cope, deal with change and live again.

◇ can change—and enjoy it!

Adapted from: *Planning, Conducting, and Evaluating Workshops* by Larry Nolan Davis and Earl McCallon, Ph.D, Learning Concepts, 2501 N. Lamar, Austin, Texas 78705.

General Methods of Surveying Groups[25]

ADVANTAGES	LIMITATIONS	DO'S AND DON'TS
Interview: Reveals feelings, causes, and possible solutions of problems as well as facts. Affords maximum opportunity for free expression of opinion, giving of suggestions.	Is time-consuming, so can reach relatively few people. Results may be difficult to quantify. Can make subject feel he is "on the spot."	Pretest and revise interview questions as needed. Be sure interview can and does listen, doesn't judge responses. Do not use to interpret, sell, or educate.
Questionnaire: Can reach many people in short time. Is relatively inexpensive. Gives opportunity of expression without fear or embarrassment. Yields data easily summarized and reported.	Little provision for free expression of unanticipated responses. May be difficult to construct. Has limited effectiveness in getting at causes of problems and possible solutions.	Pretest and revise and form as needed. Offer and safeguard anonymity. Use only if prepared to— ◇ report findings, both favorable and unfavorable. ◇ do something about them.
Tests: Are useful as diagnostic tools to identify specific areas of deficiencies. Helpful in selecting from among potential trainees those who can most profitably be trained. Results are easy to compare and report.	Tests validated for many specific situations often not available. Tests validated elsewhere may prove invalid in new situations. Results give clues, are not conclusive. Tests are second-best evidence in relation to job performance.	Know what test measures. Be sure it is worth measuring here. Apply results only to factors for which test is good. Don't use tests to take blame for difficult or unpopular decisions which management should make.

ADVANTAGES	LIMITATIONS	DO'S AND DON'TS
Group Problems Analysis: Same as for interview plus: Permits synthesis of different viewpoints. Promotes general understanding and agreement. Builds support for needed training.	Is time-consuming and initially expensive. Supervisors and executives may feel too busy to participate, want work done for them. Results may be difficult to quantify.	Do not promise or expect quick results. Start with problem known to be of concern to group. Let group make own analysis, set own priorities. Identify all problems of significant concern to group.
Job Analysis and Performance Review: Produces specific and precise information about jobs, performance. Is directly tied to actual jobs and to on-job performance. Breaks joy into segments manageable both for training and for appraisal purposes.	Time-consuming. Difficult for people not specifically trained in job analysis techniques. Supervisors often dislike reviewing employees' inadequacies with them personally. Reveals training needs of individuals but not those based on needs of organization.	Brush up on job-analysis techniques, arrange special training for those who are to do it. Be sure analysis is of current job, and current performance. Review with employee both— ◇ analysis of job, and ◇ appraisal of performance
Records and Reports Study: Provide excellent clues to trouble spots. Provide best objective evidence of results of problems. Are usually of concern to and easily understood by operating officials.	Do not show causes of problems, or possible solutions. May not provide enough cases (e.g., grievances) to be meaningful. May not reflect current situation, recent changes.	Use as checks and clues, in combination with other methods.

Taken from: Malcolm S. Knowles, *The Modern Practice of Adult Education: From Pedagogy to Andragogy* (Chicago: Follett Publishing Company, 1980), pp. 100–101.

Evaluation Sheet for Adult Learning Programs

1. Rule number one is to have your *planning team* draw up the evaluation sheet. A team member can co-ordinate the effort and it should be part of the planning process. The basic areas to touch upon in an evaluation instrument include:
   ◇ some opportunity for positive and negative response from all participants
   ◇ brief (no longer than six questions or sections) and concise questions about the workshop/program
   ◇ quality of the presentation (avoid using a ranking system)
   ◇ stick to simple, direct and obvious questions
   ◇ allow for follow-up suggestions by participants

2. Always build time into your program for evaluation. An interesting variation on the traditional "end of the program approach" might be to have one or two question forms after the sections of the program when breaks are scheduled.

3. Always, always, always, have the team members evaluate their feelings and ideas about the program. If they do not derive a positive response from participating in the program then it will be doubly difficult for any adult leader to continue a "team approach."

4. Adult learning is just that! Avoid any program planning or evaluation techniques which are school models with adult players (evoking responses, for example by using phrases like "Raise your hands if . . . " "How many can remember what I said?" "Would you like to hang up your coats?"). There are numerous creative ways to engage participants without making them feel that someone is "in charge."

   Some hints:
   ◇ engage the group immediately in non-threatening activity or exchange
   ◇ humor is a great common factor—use it liberally but never direct it *at* anyone but yourself
   ◇ be sure to double check the appearance, ventilation, chair arrangements, etc. BEFORE you begin anything

5. Evaluation instruments are only beneficial if everyone has a chance to see the summary results of them. Too many people leave a gathering with their own impressions but seldom get a chance to see how others have reacted and benefited. Plan a few minutes to build this into the program. Applause is only one measure of success.

Self-Help Sheet for Coordination of Meetings and Programs

DID YOU .... **? ? ? ? ? ? ? ? ? ? ? ? ? ? ?**

1. *Identify:*
   —the common need or interest of the group
   —those adults in the population that you are trying to reach
   —the needs of the planners as well as the participants

2. *Develop:*
   —the topics that need addressing
   —the team approach
   —questions that evoke responses not solutions

3. *Set Goals:*
   —goals are critical to the direction of learning activity
   —goals are essential for the planning team in terms of determining the resources and techniques for a program

4. *Act Selectively:*
   —select your resource people with care
   —choose appropriate materials and aids for learning
   —include members of the intended group as resources

5. *Budget Correctly:*
   —were funds available for this project
   —were they sufficient for the scope of the project
   —if revenue was generated, have you earmarked it for future programs as follow-up

"It's easy to get there if you know where you're going." Setting goals is an integral part of all program planning. Be sure to take the time to state your goals clearly and evaluate your progress toward them throughout the process of planning.

```
┌─────────────────────────────────────────────────────────────────────────┐
│                   Sample Handout for Program Evaluation                    │
│ _____(date)                            │
│                                                                           │
│  1.  This session  _____ did  _____ did not meet my expectations.     │
│                                                                           │
│  2.  The most positive aspect of this session was:                        │
│                                                                           │
│                                                                           │
│                                                                           │
│  3.  The most negative aspect of this session was:                        │
│                                                                           │
│                                                                           │
│                                                                           │
│  4.  I would recommend that the future sessions include:                  │
│                                                                           │
│                                                                           │
│                                                                           │
│                                                                           │
│                               _____   │
│                               Name (only if you wish)                     │
└─────────────────────────────────────────────────────────────────────────┘
```

Self-Help Tool for Program Planners

Three very simple steps are critical for this self-help tool to be effective for your use:

a. Be certain that *everyone* in your planning group *uses* this sheet and answers the brief series of questions.

b. Take the time to *discuss the responses.* Just a few minutes spent on this now will save hours of communication problems in the future.

c. *Enjoy* what you are doing. Everyone in the group will have some experience of this project to share. Everyone will profit to some degree or other from working on this program. Above all else, program planning should be enjoyable.

1. Briefly write your reaction to the proposed project. (Is it a good idea? Is it a felt need in your community? Do you want to be a part of this?)

2. Did the group do what it said it would do in terms of this program?

3. What are the strengths and weaknesses of this project?

114

That's it! Keep the process simple. The old adage of What? Who? When? How? is often the best way to evaluate the program and process which you have designed. Complicated and lengthy forms are often as discouraging to participants as they are helpful for planners. Sometimes we overlook the most obvious areas which create roadblocks to an idea. The above set of questions represent the consensus approach to evaluation. Another means of evaluating a program is the evaluation by objective method. This method makes use of surveys, in-depth interviews, tests, etc. As long as the objectives of the program are clearly spelled out, those means of evaluation can be profitable.

Self-Help Tool for Planning

(Use this sheet yourself and/or with others on the planning team)

1. Write the names of the people you feel would be interested and helpful in planning this program.

2. Write out your impression of how this project might benefit others as well as yourself.

3. How much time do you have to put this project together and what would be a projected target date for implementation?

4. How can you determine if there is sufficient interest in the area for this type of activity?

5. Do you have at least three people you can personally count on to help you out with this project?

6. Write down the names of the people you would like to sound out on this idea:

```
┌─────────────────────────────────────────────────────────────────────────┐
```

Self-Help Tool for Parish Planning

Rank the following   1 (strongly)   to 10   (strongly)
                     agree   disagree

___ The parish should have a minimum of four meeting areas for adults ranging in size to accommodate groups from 12 to 200.

___ A minimum of 3% of the total parish budget should be appropriated for adult education.

___ It is the responsibility of the custodian to set up physical accommodations such as chairs, tables and microphones for parish meetings.

___ The leader of adult learning situations should have a team of parishioners to assist in the planning and implementation of adult education opportunities.

___ A priest from the parish should always be present at a parish adult education program.

___ Adult education programs sponsored by a parish should be religious in nature.

___ The adult education leader should be a professional teacher.

___ Every parish meeting should include some opportunity for prayer.

___ In adult learning situations, the program is more important than the process.

___ Adult education is a matter for professional staff planning and evaluation; therefore it should not be the sole responsibility of the director of religious education.

___ Given the varied faith levels of parishioners, adult learning programs should be wide-ranging and varied in their content, approach and appeal.

___ There should be a vehicle for a parish to recruit and involve retired persons in adult learning activities.

___ The parish staff should plan and participate as a team in a minimum of one adult education activity each year.

A Checklist for "Creating Environments"

Hospitality in a parish is a reflection of a theology of parish. The old adage "What you do speaks so loudly that I cannot hear what you say" rings especially true when it comes to adult learning environments.

1. Are there rooms available for large and small groups of adults to gather?
2. Are those areas of gathering situated in convenient locations?
3. Are the rooms properly lighted, decorated, and appointed with adult furnishings? (e.g. comfortable chairs, tables, convenient rest rooms, etc.)

Example:

The local DRE calls for a meeting with twenty-five parishioners to discuss the formation of an adult education advisory committee. The only facility is a first floor classroom with desks large enough for 8th graders, florescent lights, glass block windows, and the lingering smell of chalkdust, strong soap and pencil shavings.

Some Projected Implications:

Adults are not children and likely resent the teacher-student environment created by desks and blackboards.

There is an implied set up of "leader-workers" in lieu of collegial discussion and decision making in this environment.

It is immediately established that this parish has no adequate facility for adult learning nor does it care to provide one. The parish has spoken. "We have no money for that kind of facility."

4. Is there a budget for adult education in the parish? What proportion of the total parish budget for education is designated for adults?

5. Who is responsible for taking care of physical arrangements such as refreshments, name tags, coats, etc? Does the DRE set up chairs, plug in mikes, make the coffee and clean up?

6. How many people are involved in the *process* of adult learning?

Notes

CHAPTER I

DO WE REALLY NEED ADULT RELIGIOUS EDUCATION?

1. Marie Agnew, D.C., *Future Shapes of Adult Religious Education: A Delphi Study* (New York: Paulist Press, 1976), p. 28.

2. James R. Schaefer, "Tensions Between Adult Growth and Church Authority," *Christian Adulthood: A Catechetical Resource 82*, ed. Neil Parent (Washington, D.C.: United States Catholic Conference, 1982), pp. 21–31.

3. Leon McKenzie, *The Religious Education of Adults* (Birmingham: Religious Education Press, 1982), pp. 81, 102.

4. John L. Elias, *The Foundations and Practices of Adult Religious Education* (Malabar, Florida: Robert E. Krieger Publishing Company, 1982), pp. 107–115, 151.

5. John L. Elias, "Theoretical Foundations: Ecclesial Models of Adult Religious Education," *Christian Adulthood: A Catechetical Resource 83*, ed. Neil Parent (Washington, D.C.: United States Catholic Conference, 1983), pp. 3–9.

6. James W. Fowler, *Stages of Faith: The Psychology of Human Development and the Quest for Meaning* (San Francisco: Harper and Row, Publishers, 1981).

7. David Keirsey and Marilyn Bates, *Please Understand Me: An Essay on Temperment Styles* (Del Mar, CA: Prometheus Nemesis Books, 1978).

8. McKenzie, *The Religious Education of Adults*, pp. 100–101.

9. James Fowler, "Stages of Faith and Adult Life Cycles," *Faith Development in the Adult Life Cycle*, ed. Kenneth Stokes (New York: W. H. Sadlier, Inc., 1982), pp. 189–190.

10. Ginny Griffin, "Principles of Adult Learning," lecture given at O.I.S.E. Conference, Diocese of Steubenville, May 20, 1977.

11. *Ibid.*

12. Elias, "Theoretical Foundations: Ecclesial Models of Adult Religious Education," pp. 3–9.

13. Elias, *The Foundations and Practices of Adult Religious Education*, pp. 183–184.

CHAPTER II

EXPLORING CHRISTIAN ADULTHOOD

1. Gabriel Moran, *Education Toward Adulthood: Religion and Lifelong Learning* (New York: Paulist Press, 1979), pp. 17–35.

2. Evelyn E. Whitehead and James D. Whitehead, *Christian Life Patterns: The Psychological Challenges and Religious Invitations of Adult Life* (New York: Image Books, 1982), pp. xi–xv.

3. Carol B. Aslanian and Henry M. Brickell, *Americans in Transition: Life Changes as Reasons for Adult Learning* (New York: College Entrance Examination Board, 1980), p. 25.

4. Joan Chittister, O.S.B., "The Relationship of Stages of Human Development to Community Life," lecture given at St. Joseph Motherhouse, Cleveland, January 22, 1984.

5. Moran, pp. 28–35.

6. Gerard Egan and Michael A. Cowen, *Moving Into Adulthood: Themes and Variations of Self-Directed Development for Effective Living* (Monterey, CA: Brooks/Cole Publishing Company, 1980), pp. 2–5.

7. John L. Elias, *The Foundations and Practices of Adult Religious Education* (Malabar, Florida: Robert E. Krieger Publishing Company, 1982), p. 29.

8. Charles Bruning and Kenneth Stokes, "The Hypothesis Paper," *Faith Development in the Adult Life Cycle*, ed. Kenneth Stokes (New York: W.H. Sadlier, Inc., 1982), p. 29.

9. Whitehead, p. xv.

10. Egan, pp. 2–5.

11. *Ibid.*, pp. 4–19.

12. *Ibid.*, p. 2.

13. Aslanian, p. 27.

14. Bruning, p. 28.

15. *Ibid.*

16. Egan, pp. 3–39.

17. Bruning, p. 28.

18. Aslanian, p. 25.

19. Timothy Fallon, "Spirituality of Passage: The Gospel Vision of Wholeness," lecture given at the Eastern Region Religious Education Conference, Cleveland, April 7, 1984.

20. Bruning, p. 28.

21. Egan, pp. 3–4.

22. Aslanian, pp. 17–19.

23. Robert J. Havinghurst, *Developmental Tasks and Education*, 3rd ed. (New York: David McKay Publishing Company Inc., 1972).

24. Winston Gooden, "Responses and Comments from an Adult Developmental Perspective," *Faith Development in the Adult Life Cycle*, ed. Kenneth Stokes (New York: W.H. Sadlier, Inc., 1982), p. 89.

25. Egan, pp. 26–31.

26. Fallon.

27. Aslanian, p. 20.

28. Elias, p. 73.

29. Aslanian, p. 27.

30. Daniel Levinson, *et al.*, *The Seasons of a Man's Life* (New York: Ballantine Books, 1978).

31. Elias, pp. 9–19.

32. *Ibid.*, pp. 16–36.

33. Judy-Arin Krupp, *Adult Development: Implications for Staff Development* (Manchester, CT: Adult Development Center, 1981), pp. 15–19.

34. *Ibid.*, pp. 21–23.

35. *Ibid.*, pp. 27–31.

36. *Ibid.*, pp. 35–36.

37. *Ibid.*, pp. 41–46.

38. *Ibid.*, pp. 50–51.

39. Malcolm S. Knowles, *The Modern Practice of Adult Education: From Pedagogy to Adragogy*, rev. ed. (Chicago: Follett Publishing Company, 1980), pp. 263–264.

40. Krupp, pp. 57–62.

41. *Ibid.*, pp. 65–69.

42. *Ibid.*, pp. 75–89.

43. *Ibid.*, pp. 96–101.

44. *Ibid.*, pp. 107–109.

45. *Ibid.*, pp. 110–113.

46. Knowles, pp. 263–264.

47. Krupp, pp. 119–124.

48. *Ibid.*, pp. 127–129.

49. *Ibid.*, pp. 135–138.

50. *Ibid.*, pp. 141–142.

51. Knowles, pp. 263–264.

52. Harold W. Grant, Magdala Thompson, and Thomas E. Clark, *From Image to Likeness: A Jungian Path in the Gospel Journey* (New York: Paulist Press, 1983), pp. 13–14.

53. Whitehead, p. 47.

54. Elias, p. 68.

55. Whitehead, p. 223.

56. Elias, p. 68.

57. Bruning, p. 31.

58. Whitehead, pp. xviii–xix.

59. *Ibid.*

60. *Ibid.*

61. Bruning, p. 41.

62. Whitehead, p. 10.

63. Whitehead, p. 10.

64. *Ibid.*, p. 48.

65. *Ibid.*, pp. 17, 47–48.

66. *Ibid.*, p. 239.

67. *Ibid.*, p. 2.

68. *Ibid.*, pp. 12, 23, 24, 223, 229, 231.

69. John H. Westerhoff, III, *Inner Growth/Outer Change: An Educational Guide to Church Renewal* (New York: The Seabury Press, 1979).

70. Grant, pp. 5–14.

71. Bruning, p. 49.

72. James Dunning, "Conversion, Catechesis, and the R.C.I.A.," lecture given at the Ohio Directors of Religious Education In-Service, Columbus, March 13–14, 1982.

73. James W. Fowler, *Stages of Faith: The Psychology of Human Development and the Quest for Meaning* (San Francisco: Harper and Row, Publishers, 1981), pp. 244–245.

74. Elias, p. 67.

75. James Fowler, "Stages of Faith and Adults' Life Cycles," *Faith Development in the Adult Life Cycle*, ed. Kenneth Stokes (New York: W.H. Sadlier, Inc., 1982), p. 187.

76. Bruning, pp. 35–39.

77. Whitehead, p. xiv.

78. Elias, p. 68.

79. Fowler, *Stages of Faith*.

80. Whitehead, pp. 5, 9, 67.

81. *Ibid.*, p. 95.

82. Elias, pp. 72–74.

83. Chittister.

84. Elias, pp. 72–74.

85. *Ibid.*, p. 78.

86. *Ibid.*, pp. 77–78.

87. *Ibid.*, pp. 77–79.

88. Whitehead, p. 115.

89. Elias, pp. 78–79.

90. *Ibid.*, p. 79.

91. Chittister.

92. Whitehead, p. 131.

93. Chittister.

94. Elias, pp. 80–82.

95. Whitehead, p. 165.

96. Elias, p. 82.

97. *Ibid.*, pp. 83–84.

98. Whitehead, pp. 152–155.

99. Bruning, p. 37.

100. *Ibid.*

101. Elias, p. 85.

102. Chittister.

103. Whitehead, p. 203.

104. Elias, pp. 85–86.

105. Whitehead, p. 203.

106. Elias, p. 88.

107. *Ibid.*, p. 86.

108. *Ibid.*

109. Fowler, "Stages of Faith and Adults' Life Cycles," pp. 193–196.

110. Egan, p. 48.

111. Moran, pp. 17–36.

112. James R. Schaefer, "Tensions Between Adult Growth and Church Authority," *Christian Adulthood: A Catechetical Resource 82*, ed. Neil Parent (Washington, D.C.: United States Catholic Conference, 1982), pp. 21–31.

113. Moran, pp. 17–36.

114. Whitehead, pp. 184–186.

115. *Ibid.*, p. 201.

CHAPTER III

LIFE CYCLES AND LEARNING: NEW TRENDS IN PASSAGE

1. Carol B. Aslanian and Henry M. Brickell, *Americans in Transition: Life Changes as Reasons for Learning* (New York: College Entrance Examination Board, 1980), p. 25.

2. Malcolm S. Knowles, *The Modern Practice of Adult Education: From Pedagogy to Andragogy*, rev. ed. (Chicago: Follett Publishing Company, 1980), pp. 40–41.

3. Aslanian, p. xii.

4. *Ibid.*, p. 4.

5. *Ibid.*, pp. 3–5.

6. Cyril Houle, *The Inquiring Mind* (Madison, WI: University of Wisconsin Press, 1961).

7. Barry R. Morstain and John C. Smart, "A Motivational Typology of Adult Learners," *Journal of Higher Education* 48:6 (November/December 1977): 665–679.

8. Houle.

9. Patricia K. Cross, "A Critical Review of State and National Studies of the Needs and Interests of Adult Learners," *Adult Learning Needs and the Demand for Lifelong Learning*, ed. Charles B. Stalford (Washington, D.C.: National Institute of Education, 1978), p. 12.

10. *Ibid.*

11. Aslanian, pp. 51, 144.

12. *Ibid.*, pp. 53–55, 144.

13. *Ibid.*, pp. 55–60, 61, 144.

14. *Ibid.*, p. 89.

15. *Ibid.*, pp. 90–97, 145–152.

16. *Ibid.*, pp. 65–87, 145–152.

17. John L. Elias, *The Foundations and Practices of Adult Religious Education* (Malabar, Florida: Robert E. Krieger Publishing Company, 1982), p. 106.

18. *Ibid.*, pp. 106–107.

19. *Ibid.*, p. 105.

20. Aslanian, pp. 108–115.

21. *Ibid.*, p. 115.

22. Judy-Arin Krupp, *The Adult Learner: A Unique Entity* (Manchester, CT: Adult Development and Learning, 1982), pp. 1–3.

23. *Ibid.*, pp. 2–3.

24. Leon McKenzie, *The Religious Education of Adults* (Birmingham: Religious Education Press, 1982), p. 141.

25. Elias, p. 101.

26. Krupp, pp. 33–34, 57–61, 101, 162.

27. Patricia K. Cross, *Adults as Learners* (San Francisco: Jossey-Bass Inc., 1981), p. 184.

28. Malcolm S. Knowles, "A Theory of Christian Adult Religious Education Methodology," *Christian Adulthood: A Catechetical Resource 82*, ed. Neil Parent (Washington, D.C.: United States Catholic Conference, 1982), p. 12.

29. Krupp, pp. 186–187.

30. James J. DeBoy, "Principles and Resources for Adult Religious Learning," *P.A.C.E.* 10 (1979): 39.

31. Leon McKenzie, *Adult Religious Education: The 20th Century Challenge* (West Mystic, CT: Twenty-Third Publications, 1975), p. 42.

32. Krupp, pp. 11–13.

33. Cross, *Adults as Learners*, p. 184.

34. Krupp, pp. 184–186.

35. McKenzie, *Adult Religious Education*, p. 43.

36. Krupp, pp. 25–30, 186–187.

37. Elias, p. 103.

38. Krupp, pp. 18–25.

39. *Ibid.*, pp. 67–72, 133–136, 169–174.

40. Ginny Griffin, "Principles of Adult Learning," lecture given at the O.I.S.E. Conference, Diocese of Steubenville, May 20, 1977.

41. Krupp, pp. 136–138.

42. Knowles, "A Theory of Christian Adult Religious Education Methodology," p. 12.

43. Krupp, pp. 119–124, 136–138.

44. Cross, *Adults as Learners*, p. 184.

45. Krupp, pp. 13–17, 72–73.

46. *Ibid.*, pp. 102–110.

47. Cross, *Adults as Learners*, p. 184.

48. Deboy, p. 40.

49. Griffin.

50. Cross, *Adults as Learners*, p. 184.

51. Griffin.

52. DeBoy, p. 40.

53. Cross, *Adults as Learners*, p. 184.

54. DeBoy, p. 40.

55. Krupp, pp. 35–36, 995–99.

56. McKenzie, *Adult Religious Education*, pp. 45–46.

57. Krupp, p. 36.

58. *Ibid.*, pp. 53–58.

59. Harold W. Grant, Magdala Thompson and Thomas E. Clark, *From Image to Likeness: A Jungian Path in the Gospel Journey* (New York: Paulist Press, 1983), pp. 20–25, 215–248.

60. Krupp, pp. 53–66.

61. McKenzie, *Adult Religious Education*, p. 45.

62. DeBoy, p. 40.

63. Krupp, pp. 60–65, 177–183.

64. Griffin.

65. Krupp, pp. 74, 77–79.

66. Elias, pp. 103–104.

67. Krupp, pp. 80–83.

68. Elias, p. 103.

69. A. Gregorc, "Learning/Teaching Styles: Their Nature and Effects," *Student Learning Styles: Diagnosing and Prescribing Programs* (Reston, VA: National Association of Secondary School Principals, 1979).

70. Krupp, pp. 83–84.

71. DeBoy, p. 40.

72. Griffin.

73. McKenzie, *Adult Religious Education*, p. 46.

74. Krupp, pp. 37–41.

75. McKenzie, *Adult Religious Education*, p. 46.

76. Krupp, pp. 41–42.

77. *Ibid.*, pp. 41–42, 152–156.

78. McKenzie, *Adult Religious Education*, p. 44.

79. Griffin.

80. Deboy, p. 39.

81. McKenzie, *Adult Religious Education*, pp. 43–44.

82. DeBoy, p. 40.

83. Knowles, "A Theory of Christian Adult Religious Education Methodology," p. 12.

84. Griffin.

85. McKenzie, *Adult Religious Education*, p. 44.

86. Krupp, pp. 194–201.

87. Griffin.

88. DeBoy, p. 40.

89. Cross, *Adults as Learners*, p. 184.

90. Gabriel Moran, *Education Toward Adulthood: Religion and Lifelong Learning* (New York: Paulist Press, 1979).

91. Elias.

92. Knowles, *The Modern Practice of Adult Education: From Pedagogy to Andragogy.*

93. Malcolm S. Knowles, *Self-Directed Learning: A Guide for Learners and Teachers* (Chicago: Follett Publishing Company, 1975).

94. Malcolm S. Knowles, "An Educator's Reflections on Faith Development in the Adult Life Cycle," *Faith Development in the Adult Life Cycle*, ed. Kenneth Stokes (New York: W.H. Sadlier, Inc., 1982), pp. 63–76.

95. John Elias, "Ecclesial Models of Adult Religious Education," *Christian Adulthood: A Catechetical Resource 82*, ed. Neil Parent (Washington, D.C.: United States Catholic Conference, 1982), pp. 3–9.

96. James R. Schaefer, "Tensions Between Adult Growth and Church Authority," *Christian Adulthood: A Catechetical Resource 82*, ed. Neil Parent (Washington, D.C.: United States Catholic Conference, 1982).

97. McKenzie, *The Religious Education of Adults.*

CHAPTER IV
EDUCATING CHRISTIAN ADULTS

1. John L. Elias, *The Foundations and Practices of Adult Religious Education* (Malabar, Florida: Robert E. Krieger Publishing Company, 1982), p. 103.

2. *Ibid.*, pp. 91–92.

3. Harold W. Grant, Magdala Thompson, and Thomas E. Clark, *From Image to Likeness: A Jungian Path in the Gospel Journey* (New York: Paulist Press, 1983), pp. 1–9.

4. Gabriel Moran, *Education Toward Adulthood: Religion and Lifelong Learning* (New York: Paulist Press, 1979).

5. Evelyn E. Whitehead and James D. Whitehead, *Christian Life Patterns: The Psychological Challenges and Religious Invitations of Adult Life* (New York: Image Books, 1982), pp. xxvi–xxvii, 26.

6. Archdiocesan Office of Religious Education, *Adult Participation: Answering the Call to Minister* (Cincinnati: Archdiocese of Cincinnati, 1977).

7. *Ibid.*

8. Thomas H. Groome, *Christian Religious Education: Sharing Our Story and Vision* (San Francisco: Harper and Row, Publishers, 1980).

9. Charles Bruning and Kenneth Stokes, "The Hypothesis Paper," *Faith Development in the Adult Life Cycle*, ed. Kenneth Stokes (New York: W.H. Sadlier, Inc., 1982), pp. 40–50.

10. Whitehead, pp. 233–234.

11. Groome.

12. Leon McKenzie and Matt Hayes, "How Adults Define Faith: A Factor-Analytic Study," *The Living Light* 19 (Spring 1982):35–41.

13. Joan Chittister, O.S.B., "The Relationship of Stages of Human Development to Community Life," a lecture given at St. Joseph Motherhouse, Cleveland, January 22, 1984.

CHAPTER V

TECHNIQUES FOR EFFECTIVE ADULT EDUCATION

1. Russell D. Robinson, *An Introduction to Helping Adults Learn and Change* (Mulwake, WI: Omnibook Co., 1979), p. 89.

2. *Ibid.*, pp. 90–92.

3. *Ibid.*, pp. 92–93.

4. *Ibid.*, p. 94.

5. *Ibid.*, p. 95.

6. *Ibid.*, pp. 70–71.

7. *Ibid.*, p. 71.

8. *Ibid.*, p. 72.

9. Malcolm S. Knowles, *The Modern Practice of Adult Education: From Pedagogy to Andragogy*, rev. ed. (Chicago: Follett Publishing Company, 1980), pp. 236–237.

10. Donald L. Griggs, *Teaching Teachers To Teach* (Nashville: Abingdon Press, 1974), pp. 17–22.

11. Mary K. Cove, S.S.J. and Jane E. Regan, *TREP: Teaching Religion Effectively Program* (Dubuque, Iowa: Wm. C. Brown Company Publishers, 1982), pp. 29–31.

12. Griggs, pp. 24–25.

13. Robinson, p. 97.

14. Knowles, pp. 164–165.

15. Diocese of Youngstown, *Aspirgrow Consultant Training Handbook* (Youngstown: Diocese of Youngstown, 1978), p. 40.

16. Malcolm S. Knowles, *The Modern Practice of Adult Education: From Pedagogy to Andragogy*, rev. ed. (Chicago: Follett Publishing Company, 1980), p. 240.

17. Bernice McCarthy, "Learning Styles in Education," lecture given at Southern Region Office, Diocese of Cleveland, Akron, April 1983.

18. *Ibid.*

19. A. Gregorc, "Learning and Teaching Styles: Their Nature and Effects," *Student Learning Styles: Diagnosing and Prescribing Programs* (Reston, VA, National Association of Secondary School Principals, 1979).

20. Judy-Arin Krupp, *The Adult Learner: A Unique Entity* (Manchester, CT: Adult Development and Learning, 1982).

21. Bernice McCarthy.

22. Donnie Dutton, "Should the Clientele Be Involved in Program Planning?" *Adult Leadership* (December 1970), p. 2.

23. James Schaefer, *Program Planning for Adult Christian Education* (New York: Newman Press, 1972), pp. 34–50.

24. Larry Nolan Davis and Earl McCallon, Ph.D., *Planning, Conducting and Evaluating Workshops* (Austin, TX: Learning Concepts).

25. Knowles, pp. 100–101.

Selected Bibliography

Academy for Educational Development. *Never Too Old To Learn.* New York: Academy for Educational Development, Inc., 1974.

Agnew, Marie, D.C. *Future Shapes of Adult Religious Education: A Delphi Study.* New York: Paulist Press, 1976.

Archdiocesan Office of Religious Education. *Adult Participation: Answering the Call To Minister.* Cincinnati: Archdiocese of Cincinnati, 1977.

Aslanian, Carol B., and Henry M. Brickell. *Americans in Transition: Life Changes as Reasons for Learning.* New York: College Entrance Examination Board, 1980.

Asslelin, Paul, C.P.S. "Process Planning and Adult Education." *Institute for Continuing Education Handbook.* Detroit: Archdiocese of Detroit, 1977.

Astley, Jeff. "The Role of Worship in Christian Learning." *Religious Education.* 79 (Spring 1984): 243–251.

Bader, Diana, "Adult Learning: Preparing the Leaders." *P.A.C.E.* 8 (1977): 1–2.

Bergevin, Paul. "On Adult Learners." *Institute for Continuing Education Handbook.* Detroit: Archdiocese of Detroit, 1977.

Berginn, Paul, Dwight Monis, and Robert Smith. *Adult Education Procedures: A Handbook of Tested Patterns.* New York: The Seabury Press, 1963.

Bloom, Benjamin S., ed. *Taxonomy of Educational Objectives Handbook I: Cognitive Domain.* New York: David McKay Company, Inc., 1956.

Bosio, John. "A Day of Sharing in Adult Religious Education." *P.A.C.E.* 6 (1975): 1–2.

Breidenbach, Monica. "Please Touch: A Parish Do-It-Yourself Adult Education Program." *P.A.C.E.* 8 (1977): 1–3.

Brennan, Patrick. "Recycling and Reentering the Church: Evangelization and Lapsed Catholics," *Christian Initiation Resources,* Vol. 1. New York: Wm. Sadlier Inc., 1981.

Bruning, Charles, and Kenneth Stokes. "The Hypothesis Paper." *Faith Development in the Adult Life Cycle,* ed. Kenneth Stokes. New York: W.H. Sadlier, Inc., 1982, pp. 17–61.

Burghardt, Walter J. *Seasons That Laugh or Weep: Musings on the Human Journey.* New York: Paulist Press, 1983.

Cardman, Francine. "On Spirituality and Religious Education." *P.A.C.E.* 14 (1983): 1–3.

Casper, Martin. "Religious Education Programs for Older Adults." *Institute for Continuing Education Handbook.* Detroit: Archdiocese of Detroit, 1977.

Chittister, Joan, O.S.B. "The Relationship of the Stages of Human Development and Community Life," a lecture given at St. Joseph Motherhouse, Cleveland, January 22, 1984.

Clift, Wallace B. *Jung and Christianity: The Challenge of Reconciliation.* New York: Crossroad Publishing Company, 1982.

Cove, Mary K. and Jane E. Regan. *TREP: Teaching Religion Effectively Program.* Dubuque, Iowa: Wm. C. Brown Company Publishers, 1982.

Cove, Mary K. and Mary Louise Mueller. *Regarding Religious Education.* Mishawaka, IN: Religious Education Press, 1977.

Crawford, Margaret A. and Matthew J. Hayes. "A Decentralized Approach to Parish Adult Religious Education." *P.A.C.E.* 11 (1981): 1–3.

Cronin, Joan. "Implications for Adult Religious Education." *Faith Development in the Adult Life Cycle*, ed. Kenneth Stokes. New York: W.H. Sadlier, Inc., 1982, pp. 291–295.

Cross, Patricia K. "A Critical Review of State and National Studies of the Needs and Interests of Adult Learners." *Adult Learning Needs and the Demand for Lifelong Learning*, ed. Charles B. Stalford. Washington, D.C.: National Institute of Education, 1978.

Cross, Patricia K. *Adults as Learners*. San Francisco: Jossey-Bass Inc., 1981.

Cummings, James and Lynn Cummings. "Publicity Pays Off." *Today's Parish* (January 1984): 24–26.

Davis, Larry Nolan and Earl McCallon, Ph.D. *Planning, Conducting, and Evaluating Workshops*. Austin, TX: Learning Concepts.

DeBoy, James J. "Principles and Resources for Adult Religious Learning." *P.A.C.E.* 10 (1979): 39–42.

Deer, R.L. *A Taxonomy of Social Purposes of Public Schools*. New York: David McKay Company, Inc., 1973.

Department of Education. *Moral Education and Christian Conscience: Value Education in Perspective*. Washington, D.C.: United States Catholic Conference, 1977.

Diocese of Youngstown. *Aspirgrow Consultant Training Handbook*. Youngstown: Diocese of Youngstown, 1978.

Downs, Thomas. *A Journey to Self Through Dialogue: An Excursion of Spiritual Self-Discovery for Individuals and Groups*. West Mystic, CT: Twenty-Third Publications, 1977.

Duggan, Robert. "Conversion: Toward a Better Understanding." *The Living Light* 18 (Fall 1981): 216–224.

Dunning, James. "Conversion, Catechesis and the R.C.I.A.," a lecture given at the Ohio Directors of Religious Education Conference, Columbus, March 13–14 1982.

Dunning, James. *Ministries: Sharing God's Gifts*. Winona, Minn.: St. Mary's Press, 1980.

Dutton, Donnie, Ph.D. "Should the Clientele Be Involved in Program Planning?" *Adult Leadership* (December 1970): 1–4.

Egan, Gerard and Michael A. Cowen. *Moving Into Adulthood: Themes and Variations in Self-Directed Development for Effective Living*. Monterey, CA: Brooks/Cole Publishing Company, 1980.

Elias, John L. "Ecclesial Models of Adult Religious Education." *Christian Adulthood: A Catechetical Resource 82*, ed. Neil Parent Washington, D.C.: United States Catholic Conference, 1982.

Elias, John L. *The Foundations and Practices of Adult Religious Education*. Malabar, FL: Robert E. Krieger Publishing Company, 1982.

Engels, John J. "Myths and Needs of Young Adults." *P.A.C.E.* 10 (1979): 1–4.

Griggs, Donald L. *Teaching Teachers To Teach*. Nashville: Abingdon Press, 1980.

Fallon, Timothy. "Spirituality of Passage: The Gospel Vision of Wholeness," a lecture given at Eastern Region Religious Education Conference, Diocese of Cleveland, April 7, 1984.

Flood, Edward. "For an Adult Church." *Tablet* 235 (June 13, 1981): 270–271.

Fowler, James. "Stages of Faith and Adults' Life Cycles." *Faith Development in the Adult Life Cycle*, ed. Kenneth Stokes. New York: W.H. Sadlier, Inc., 1982, pp. 179–207.

Fowler, James. *Stages of Faith: The Psychology of Human Development and the Quest for Meaning*. San Francisco: Harper and Row, Publishers, 1981.

Fowler, James, and Antoine Vergote *et al. Toward Moral and Religious Maturity: The First International Conference on Moral and Religious Development*, convenor Christiane Brusselmans. Morristown, N.J.: Silver Burdett Company, 1980.

Friend, William B. "Transformation Through Holistic Spirituality and Ministry." *The Living Light* 20 (January 1984): 152–158.

Futrell, John Carroll. "Growing Older Gracefully." *Human Development* 3 (Fall 1982): 6–12.

Gooden, Winston. "Responses and Comments from an Adult Developmental Perspective." *Faith Development in the Adult Life Cycle*, ed. Kenneth Stokes. New York: W.H. Sadlier, Inc., 1982, pp. 85–119.

Grant, Harold W., Magdala Thompson, and Thomas E. Clark. *From Image to Likeness: Jungian Path in the Gospel Journey*. New York: Paulist Press, 1983.

Gregorc, A. "Learning and Teaching Styles: Their Nature and Effects." *Student Learning Styles: Diagnosing and Prescribing Programs*. Reston: VA: National Association of Secondary School Principals, 1979.

Gribbon, R.T. "Faith Development Theory: A Tool For Ministry." *Alban Institute Action Information Newsletter* 8, no. 3 (1981): 6–8.

Griffin, Ginny. "Principles of Adult Learning," a lecture given at the O.I.S.E. Conference, Steubenville Diocese of Ohio, May 20, 1977.

Griggs, Donald. *Teaching Teachers To Teach*. Abingdon Press, 1974, pp. 17–22.

Groome, Thomas H. *Christian Religious Education: Sharing Our Story and Vision*. San Francisco: Harper and Row, Publishers, 1980.

Gross, Ronald. *A Handbook for the Lifelong Learner*. New York: Simon and Schuster, 1977.

Halon, Kevin. "Adulthood and Catechesis." *Month* 15 (July 1982): 235–241.

Harris, Maria. "The Religious Educator as a Spiritual Director." *P.A.C.E.* 8 (1977): 1–4.

Hater, Robert J. *Religious Education and Catechesis: A Shift in Focus*. Washington, D.C.: National Conference of Diocesan Directors of Religious Education, 1981.

Hater, Robert J. *The Relationship Between Evangelization and Catechesis*. Washington, D.C.: National Conference of Diocesan Directors of Religious Education, 1981.

Havinghurst, R.J. *Developmental Tasks and Education*, 3rd ed. New York: David McKay Company, Inc., 1972.

Hayes, Matthew J. "The Many Advantages of Small Group Learning." *P.A.C.E.* 8 (1977): 1-4.

Henry, Norbert. "Adult Education Cabaret Style." *P.A.C.E.* 6 (1975): 1–2.

Hill, Marie, Brennan Hill. *Adult Catechesis: Basic Parish Programs*. Winona, Minn.: St. Mary's College Press, 1977.

Houle, Cyril. *The Design of Education*. San Francisco: Jossey-Bass Publishers, 1978.

Houle, Cyril. *The Inquiring Mind*. Madison, WI: University of Wisconsin Press, 1961.

Husson, William. "A Practical Model for Adult Biblical Learning." *Religious Education* 77 (September/October 1982): 534–539.

Hughes, Jane Wolford, ed. *Ministering to Adult Learners: A Skills Workbook for Christian Education Leaders*. Washington, D.C.: United States Catholic Conference, 1981.

Johnson, Paul. "Faith Stances, Imagination, and Campus Ministry." *Faith Development in the Adult Life Cycle*, ed. Kenneth Stokes. New York: W.H. Sadlier, Inc., 1982, pp. 245–263.

Keirsey, David, and Marilyn Bates. *Please Understand Me: An Essay on Temperament Styles*. Del Mar, CA: Prometheus Nemesis Press, 1978.

Kelly, Francis D. "Adult Learning and the Modern Parish." *Momentum* (May 1984): 25–26.

Kelsey, Morton. *Can Christians Be Educated?* Mishawaka, IN: Religious Education Press Inc., 1977.

Kidd, J.R. *How Adults Learn*. New York: Association Press, 1973.

Kirwin, Patricia M. "The New Era of Adult Religious Education: Knowing Where the Tigers Are." *Momentum* (May 1984): 18–20.

Klevins, Chester. *Materials and Methods in Adult Education*. New York: Klevins Publications, 1972.

Knowles, Malcolm S. "An Adult Educator's Reflections on Faith Development in the Adult Life Cycle." *Faith Development in the Adult Life Cycle*, ed. Kenneth Stokes. New York: W.H. Sadlier, Inc., 1982, pp. 63–83.

Knowles, Malcolm S. "A Theory of Christian Adult Religious Education Methodology." *Christian Adulthood: A Catechetical Resource 82*, ed. Neil Parent. Washington, D.C.: United States Catholic Conference, 1982, pp. 9–16.

Knowles, Malcolm S. *Self-Directed Learning: A Guide For Learners and Teachers*. Chicago: Follett Publishing Company, 1975.

Knowles, Malcolm S. *The Modern Practice of Adult Education: From Pedagogy to Andragogy*, rev. ed. Chicago: Follett Publishing Company, 1980.

Koob, Albert. "Making the Way Smooth for Lay Leadership." *Momentum* (May 1984): 23–25.

Kraft, William F. "Spiritual Growth in Adolescence and Adulthood." *Human Development* 4 (Winter 1983): 14–23.

Krathwohl, David, Benjamin S. Bloom, and B. Masis. *Taxonomy of Educational Objectives Handbook II: Affective Domain*. New York: David McKay Company, Inc., 1964.

Krupp, Judy-Arin. *Adult Development: Implications for Staff Development*. Manchester, CT: Adult Development and Learning, 1981.

Krupp, Judy-Arin. *The Adult Learner: A Unique Entity*. Manchester, CT: Adult Development and Learning, 1982.

Lasker, Harry, James Moore, and Edwin L. Simpson. *Adult Development and Approaches to Learning*. Washington, D.C.: U.S. Government Printing Office, 1980.

Levinson, Daniel J. *et al. The Seasons of a Man's Life*. New York: Ballantine Books, 1978.

Leypoldt, Martha M. *Learning Is Change: Adult Education in the Church*. Valley Forge, PA: Judson Press, 1971.

Maher, Mary. "Using Sunday's Scripture Readings with Adult Groups." *P.A.C.E.* 8 (1977): 1–4.

Matthews, George. "Some Implications for Andragogy." *Institute For Continuing Education Handbook*. Detroit: Archdiocese of Detroit, 1977.

McBride, Alfred A., O.Praem. *Creative Teaching in Christian Education*. Boston: Allyn and Bacon, Inc., 1978.

McCarthy, Bernice. "Learning Styles and Education," a lecture given at the Southern Regional Office of the Diocese of Cleveland, Akron, April 1983.

McCoy, Vivian R. "Adult Life Cycle Change." *Lifelong Learning: The Adult Years* 1 (October 1977): 14–18, 31.

McCoy, Vivian Rogers. "Adult Life Cycle Change Tasks/Adult Continuing Education Response." *The Adult Life Cycle: A Training Manual and Reader*, ed. Vivian Rogers McCoy, *et al.* Lawrence, KA: Adult Life Resource Center, University of Kansas, 1978.

McElreth, Mark P. "How To Figure Out What Adults Want To Know." *Institute for Continuing Education Handbook*. Detroit: Archdiocese of Detroit, 1977.

McGrath, Francis. *Parish Adult Religious Education: The Ten Commandments of Parish Adult Education*. Glenwood, IL: Alexander Services, date unknown.

McKenzie, Leon. *Adult Religious Education: The 20th Century Challenge*. West Mystic, CT: Twenty-Third Publications, 1975.

McKenzie, Leon. "Foundations: The Scope, Purpose, and Goals of Adult Religious Education." *Christian Adulthood: A Catechetical Resource 82*, ed. Neil Parent. Washington, D.C.: United States Catholic Conference, 1982, pp. 17–20.

McKenzie, Leon. *The Religious Education of Adults*. Birmingham, AL: Religious Education Press, 1982.

McKenzie, Leon and Matthew Hayes. "How Adults Define Faith: A Factor-Analytic Study." *The Living Light* 19 (Spring 1982): 35–41.

Merrifield, Charles W., ed. *Leadership in Voluntary Enterprise*. New York: Oceana Publications, 1961.

Moran, Gabriel. *Education Toward Adulthood: Religion and Lifelong Learning*. New York: Paulist Press, 1979.

Morstain, Barry R. and John C. Smart. "A Motivational Typology of Adult Learners." *Journal of Higher Education* 48 (November/December 1977): 665–679.

Murphy, Sheila. "Women Emerging From Midlife Transition." *Human Development* 4 (Spring 1983): 14–20.

Neumann, Mathias, O.S.B. "The Dynamics of Liturgy: Life-Symbols, Imagination, and Mystery." *The Living Light* 19 (Winter 1982): 318–324.

Neville, Gwen Kennedy and John H. Westerhoff, III. *Learning Through Liturgy*. New York: The Seabury Press, 1978.

Perlinski, Jerome. "Christians in Search: A Possible Model in Adult Education." *P.A.C.E.* 6 (1975): 1–4.

Poly, Kenneth. "Life-Situation Learning." *P.A.C.E.* 6 (1975): 1–3.

Reber, Robert E. "Some Key Principles for Guiding Adult Education Programs." *Institute for Continuing Education Handbook*. Detroit: Archdiocese of Detroit, 1977.

Robinson, Russell D. *An Introduction to Helping Adults Learn and Change*. Mulwake, WI: Omnibook Company, 1979.

Ross, Robert W. "Transadulthood: New Thoughts on Older Youth." *P.A.C.E.* 6 (1975): 1–3.

Scapanski, Gene. "How To Make Adult Programs a Success." *Ministries* (February 1981): 13–33.

Schaefer, James. *GIFT: Growth in Faith Together*. New York: Paulist Press, 1973.

Schaefer, James. *Program Planning for Adult Christian Education*. New York: Newman Press, 1972.

Schaefer, James. "Tensions Between Adult Growth and Church Authority." *Christian Adulthood: A Catechetical Resource 82*, ed. Neil Parent. Washington, D.C.: United States Catholic Conference, 1982, pp. 22–32.

Schaefer, James. "Questions To Ask Before Planning a Program." *P.A.C.E.* 1 (1970): 1–3.

Sheehy, Gail. *Passages: Predictable Crises of Adult Life*. New York: Bantam Books, 1976.

Shere, James M. "Three Challenges for Adult Education." Source unknown.

Sixeas, Virginia. "Toward Practicing What We Preach: A Reflective Group Process." *P.A.C.E.* 11 (1980): 1–4.

Smith, Gregory Michael. "Integrating Life's Experiences Religious Education." *Momentum* (May 1984): 20–22.

Stokes, Kenneth. "Faith Development in the Adult Life Cycle/Adult Ministry in the Church," a lecture series given at St. Meinrad School of Theology, St. Meinrad, IN, January 15–21, 1984.

Stowe, Connie Rae. "What About Adult Religious Education?" *C.A.R.E.* Cleveland: Diocese of Cleveland, 1979.

Torrens, James, S.J. "Mostly It Takes Years." *Human Development* 3 (Summer 1982): 36–38.

Trester, Eugene F. "Adult Biblical Learning in Community." *Religious Education* 77 (September/October 1982): 540–547.

United States Catholic Conference. *Sharing the Light of Faith: National Catechetical Directory for Catholics in the United States*. Washington: D.C.: Department of Education, United States Catholic Conference, 1979.

Vogel, Linda Jane. *The Religious Education of Older Adults*. Birmingham, AL: Religious Education Press, 1984.

Walsh, Kathleen and Michael Walsh. "Problems in Adult Religious Education." *Month* 16 (May 1983): 92–96.

Westerhoff, John H., III. *Inner Growth/Outer Change: An Educational Guide to Church Renewal*. New York: The Seabury Press, 1979.

Westley, Dick. *Redemptive Intimacy: A New Perspective for the Journey of Adult Faith*. Mystic, CT: Twenty-Third Publications, 1981.

Whitehead, Evelyn and James D. Whitehead. *Christian Life Patterns: The Psychological Challenges and Religious Invitations of Adult Life*. New York: Image Books, 1982.

268.434
Sz 99

Lincoln Christian College

74672